NEEDS ASSESSMENT
Basics

DEBORAH TOBEY

A Complete, How-to Guide to Help You:

- Ensure Performance and Bottom-line Impact

- Guarantee Organization and Individual Relevance

- Gain Commitment to Process

ASTD Press

D1300546

14 13 12 11 10   3 4 5 6 7 8

ASTD Press is an internationally renowned source of insightful and practical information on workplace learning and performance topics, including training basics, evaluation and return-on-investment (ROI), instructional systems development (ISD), e-learning, leadership, and career development.

Ordering information: Books published by ASTD Press can be purchased by visiting our website at store.astd.org or by calling 800.628.2783 or 703.683.8100.

Library of Congress Control Number: 2004116267

ISBN-10: 1-56286-387-8
ISBN-13: 978-1-56286-387-6

Acquisitions and Development Editor: Mark Morrow
Copyeditor: Karen Eddleman
Interior Design and Production: Kathleen Schaner
Cover Design: Ana Ilieva
Cover Illustration: Phil and Jim Bliss

All tables and figures printed with permission of DEB TOBEY LLC.

Table of Contents

About the
Training Basics Series

STD's *Training Basics* series recognizes and, in some ways, celebrates the fast-paced, ever-changing reality of organizations today. Jobs, roles, and expectations change quickly. One day you might be a network administrator or a process line manager, and the next day you might be asked to train 50 employees in basic computer skills or to instruct line workers in quality processes.

Where do you turn for help? The ASTD *Training Basics* series is designed to be your one-stop solution. The series takes a minimalist approach to your learning curve dilemma and presents only the information you need to be successful. Each book in the series guides you through key aspects of training: giving presentations, making the transition to the role of trainer, designing and delivering training, and evaluating training. The books in the series also include some advanced skills such as performance and basic business proficiencies.

The ASTD *Training Basics* series is the perfect tool for training and performance professionals looking for easy-to-understand materials that will prepare non-trainers to take on a training role. In addition, this series is the perfect reference tool for any trainer's bookshelf and a quick way to hone your existing skills. The titles currently planned for the series include:

- ▸ *Presentation Basics* (2003)
- ▸ *Trainer Basics* (2003)
- ▸ *Training Design Basics* (2003)
- ▸ *Facilitation Basics* (2004)
- ▸ *Communication Basics* (2004)
- ▸ *Performance Basics* (2004)
- ▸ *Evaluation Basics* (2005)
- ▸ *Needs Assessment Basics* (2005)
- ▸ *ROI Basics* (2005)
- ▸ *Organization Development Basics* (2005).

Preface

This book is for training professionals—instructional designers, trainers, or training department managers—who want to make sure that their training programs meet the performance needs of their organizations. If you're reading this book, it's likely that your goals are to develop the foundation that will ensure the training programs you design and deliver will

- ▶ have a bottom-line impact on the business needs of your organization
- ▶ ensure that employee performance on the job contributes to that impact
- ▶ make certain that the ultimate training design is skill-based to support employee performance back on the job
- ▶ guarantee that the training delivery and facilitation are attuned to the learning needs of the participants and support an environment of learning.

The purpose of this book is to increase your understanding and experience with conducting training needs assessments and, even more important, to gain your commitment to using needs assessment as the foundation for effective training design, development, delivery, and evaluation.

One caveat: You will notice that the assumption in this book is that the reader is an internal training staff person in an organization. If you are an external trainer/consultant, these methods will work for you as well. Any special considerations for external consultants are highlighted along the way.

I dedicate this book to my husband, Bryan Tobey, and my parents, Barbara and Dale Davis. My sincere thanks go to my friend and colleague Don McCain for his continuing support, listening ear, and suggestions. And, to all of my colleagues over the years whose interaction has stimulated and buoyed me, thanks to you most of all!

Deb Tobey
April 2005

Why Needs Assessment?

What's Inside This Chapter

In this chapter, you'll learn:

▶ Definitions of some important terms
▶ The purposes of training needs assessment
▶ The phases in training needs assessment
▶ How training needs assessment sets the stage for training evaluation
▶ How to locate information in the book using a chapter-by-chapter outline
▶ How to use the icons as a guide to special material in the book.

Introduction: An Analogy

Do you remember the old story about coal miners using canaries to test the atmosphere when they were down in the mines? It's true. In centuries past, miners took canaries or other small birds into the mines with them. Poisonous gases like carbon monoxide and methane can be released during work underground, and a canary's respiratory system is more sensitive to these toxic gases than a human's. The canary acted like an early warning system, and if the bird had trouble breathing or died, the miners knew to get out of the mine quickly. Thanks to the canary, the miners could get out of the mine alive before the poisonous gases overcame them.

Sometimes, however, the canary itself was not so fortunate. Because its respiratory system is more sensitive than the humans', the canary was often overcome by the fumes before its cage made it to the surface.

At the earliest sign of trouble, the canary was the first to go. In some ways this story is an analogy for the internal training function and its ability to conduct needs assessment effectively and efficiently. By the end of this chapter, you will know why this analogy is so apt.

What Is Training Needs Assessment?

Simply put, training needs assessment is the process of identifying how training can help your organization reach its goals. It has been referred to as "the art and science of finding the right problems and understanding them fully" (Zemke & Kramlinger, 1982). It's interesting that the words "training" or "skills" or "learning" do not appear in that definition. Yes, needs assessment does help training professionals provide input for the ultimate training design, and that is an important aspect. Even more important in needs assessment, however, is establishing that there is a business need, driving a performance need, driving a true training need, identifying the specifics regarding the desired training, and finally, identifying the non-training issues that are also present and affecting the performance situation.

Although training itself certainly provides skills and learning and development, training needs assessment is the preliminary process that ensures that training is grounded in the needs of the organization. Without needs assessment, trainers risk developing and delivering training that does not support organizational needs and, therefore, does not deliver value to the organization or the client. And, the training that is developed may not be accepted by the target audience.

Implementing a proper training needs assessment helps the organization see the value of the training function and its role as a business partner. By establishing a collaborative relationship with the client during needs assessment, a pattern of involvement and joint decision making is developed that can continue throughout the entire design, delivery, and evaluation steps of the whole training process.

Defining Key Terms

Before beginning an in-depth examination of training needs assessment, two terms that are used throughout this book must be defined: needs assessor and client.

A needs assessor may be a training, human resource development (HRD), or human resources (HR) staff member of an organization who is responsible for the design and delivery of training interventions and is, therefore, responsible for training needs assessment. Alternatively, a needs assessor may be an external training, HRD, or HR professional who works with client organizations to design and deliver training. Anyone reading this book is probably a needs assessor—or will be! In this book, the term "needs assessor" is used when referring to the individual in his or her strict role within the needs assessment process. If a more general or universal comment is necessary, the term "training professional" is used.

The client is the individual that the needs assessor is working with to design and develop training. That individual might be a department manager, a department head, or the chief executive officer (CEO). Think of the client as the person who will benefit most from the increased performance of the employees who will participate in training. On occasion, an internal professional might have an additional client: his or her own manager. For example, if you work in HR and the HR director (the boss) is driving the training project or is invested in the outcome in some way, the HR director would also be the client. And, yes, that means you would be working for two clients.

Purposes of Training Needs Assessment

Training needs assessment, when implemented effectively, serves multiple purposes:

1. It places the training need or request in the context of the organization's needs. Training adds value only when it ultimately serves a business need.
2. It validates and augments the initial issues presented by the client. Clients know their business, no doubt about it! But, sometimes they don't know the cause or the remedy for issues that involve human performance. The needs assessment can reveal different information, provide broader context for the information supplied by the client, and offer different perspectives on the client's initial impressions.
3. It ensures that the ultimate training design supports employee performance and thereby helps the organization meet its needs. A significant portion of

training needs assessment encompasses gathering information to support the training design, identify and capture skills and knowledge, and ensure that the design replicates the learners' jobs as closely as possible.

4. It results in recommendations regarding non-training issues that are affecting the achievement of the desired organization and employee performance goals. The main question is this: If the ultimate training program is perfect, what else is going on in the organization that will result in the business needs not being met? It is critical that the needs assessor identify these issues and provide recommendations to rectify them for several reasons. First, there is a much greater likelihood of achieving desired business and performance results. Second, the training function is held accountable for only the portion of the business and performance needs that it can affect. Third, it increases the value added by the training function to the organization.

Think About This

Training recommendations can also include a return-on-investment (ROI) forecast. This is a prediction of the comparison between the costs of designing/developing/delivering the training, and the value of the ultimate expected business outcome that the training is expected to influence. Clients use the ROI forecast to help them decide if a training project is worthwhile; trainers use it to influence the client's decision. ROI is dealt with briefly in this book as a possible needs assessment outcome/recommendation. It is covered in much greater detail as an evaluation technique in another volume of this series, *Evaluation Basics* (McCain, 2005).

5. It helps ensure survival of the training function. When a training program adds value, the training function is valued for its impact and results and is not at high risk during hard times. (Now do you know why the canary in the coal mine is an apt analogy?)

6. It establishes the foundation for back-end evaluation. Although this book is about front-end needs assessment, rather than back-end measurement and evaluation, the relationship between the two is very clear. Figure 1-1 illustrates how needs assessment sets the stage for evaluation. During training

Figure 1-1. Needs assessment sets the stage for evaluation.

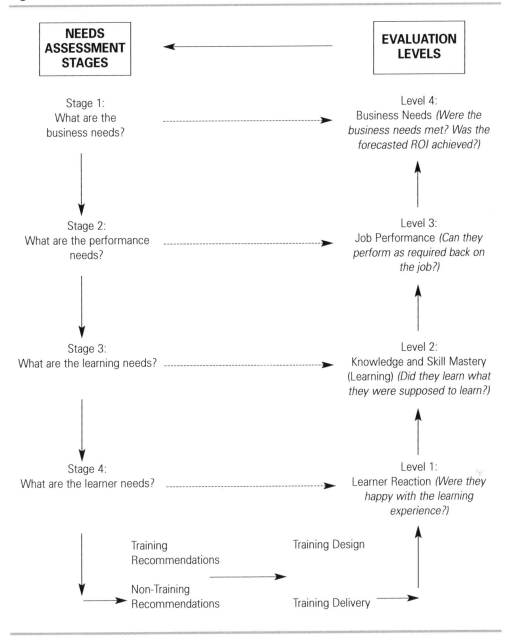

needs assessment, measures are taken at four stages (left side of figure 1-1): business needs, performance needs, learning needs, and learner needs. During evaluation (after training), measurements are taken of the very same items, now called the four levels of evaluation: learner reaction, learning (knowledge and skill mastery), job performance, and business needs. The goal in training is to be able to identify positive changes in each of the four needs assessment pre-measures when they are post-measured during evaluation. Note that after the evaluation business measurement is taken, it can result in the beginning of a new needs assessment.

Basic Rule 1
Needs assessment measures set the foundation for evaluation measures.

Noted

It's not that evaluation can't be implemented for training interventions for which no needs assessment was conducted. Back-end evaluation measures can still be taken, and the trainer and client can agree on whether or not the back-end measures meet expectations. A more powerful case for organization and performance improvement (not to mention for training itself) is made by matching the needs identified up front with the measures taken at the end, because it demonstrates impact that can be directly attributed to training. This match-up demonstrates training's added value in a very potent way.

Steps in Training Needs Assessment
The seven steps in training needs assessment are depicted in figure 1-2 and described in some detail in the following sections.

Step 1. External and Internal Organizational Scan
Training professionals spend a significant amount of time scanning the internal and external environment, gathering information from many sources: newspapers, current events, annual reports, financial statements, customer service data, strategic plans, benchmarking, and the break room, to name a few.

Figure 1-2. The training needs assessment process.

Step 1. Conduct external and organization scan

Step 2. Collect data to identify business needs

Capitalize on an opportunity
Resolve a problem
Support a strategy

Step 3. Identify potential training intervention

Step 4. Collect data to identify performance, learning, and learner needs

Required performance
Learners' current performance
Required skills and knowledge
Learners' current skills and knowledge
Learner needs

Step 5. Analyze data

Identify findings: gaps in performance, skills, and knowledge
Identify recommendations

Step 6. Deliver data analysis feedback

Training recommendations: design and delivery; ROI forecast
Non-training recommendations: work environment, rewards, consequences, work processes

Transition step: Begin training design

Step 2. Collect Data to Identify Business Needs

From the scanning process, the needs assessor is able to identify the current organizational needs. Organizational needs fall into three categories:

▹ an opportunity that must be capitalized upon (for example, a new product or new market)
▹ a problem that must be resolved (for example, waste, customer complaints, poor product quality, absenteeism)
▹ a business strategy that must be supported (for example, a marketing and product approach that caters to a certain age group, or a hospital that wants to brand itself as "the maternity hospital in the community").

Business needs can be identified at the macro level (the overall organization) or at the micro level (one department or unit, depending on whom your client is).

Step 3. Identify Potential Training Intervention

At this point in the process, potential training interventions have usually been identified by either the needs assessor or the client. Sometimes the needs assessor approaches the client to share discoveries that have been made during organizational scanning, and sometimes the client makes the first move.

Step 4. Collect Data to Identify Performance, Learning, and Learner Needs

Multiple sources of data must be addressed to identify desired and current job performance, desired and current skill/knowledge level, and learner needs. Each set of needs is likely to include both skill deficiencies (training needs) and other issues that affect performance (non-training needs).

Step 5. Analyze Data

Data analysis yields findings that identify the gaps between desired and current job performance, and between desired and current knowledge/skill levels, so that the ultimate training design will target those gaps. Understanding the magnitude of these gaps also assists the needs assessor in assigning priorities to the various issues that have to be addressed.

Step 6. Deliver Data Analysis Feedback

The needs assessor makes a presentation or generates a report for the client detailing findings, training recommendations for design and delivery, and non-training recommendations (recommendations to resolve issues that are not caused by skill deficiencies).

Transition Step: Begin Training Design Process

This is where the process segues into design. If the needs assessment has been implemented well, the training designer has ample information to produce targeted learning objectives, learning activities, job-relevant content and materials to support activities, measurement and evaluation tools, and a learning environment.

Each of these steps is explored more fully in later chapters. For now, however, notice that this process includes two steps that occur before a training intervention is even mentioned. It is critical that any training undertaken be directly linked to the business needs of the organization through internal and external scanning and identification of business needs before any other work is done. If not, value is not added. If value is not added and the organization hits a rough spot, functions that haven't added any value are at the highest risk.

Basic Rule 2

Training needs assessment results in training that supports business needs first and, in so doing, adds value to the organization.

Chapter-by-Chapter Highlights

To successfully assess training needs, you need to be able to identify the context for a training course request at four separate stages. You also must be able to identify the big picture of training needs throughout the organization. This book can help you do that. Here's a summary of the 10 chapters in *Needs Assessment Basics*:

1. "Why Needs Assessment?" This introductory chapter gives you an overview of the book. It focuses on the multiple purposes of needs assessment and serves as a roadmap to the rest of the book.
2. "The Training Request" shows you how to begin to analyze training needs assessment within the most common framework encountered by trainers: receiving a training request from a client/manager in your organization. You will learn about the four stages of data collection required for thorough needs assessment and about the challenge of creating internal credibility so that you can conduct your needs assessment.
3. "Identifying Questions and Data Sources" helps you identify questions that must be answered by needs assessment. And, you will identify the sources that will provide the needed data.

4. "Evaluating Potential Data Collection Methods" offers guidance on how to choose data collection methods to answer the identified questions using the selected data sources. When comparing data collection methods, you must consider time and resource constraints and realize that certain methods work best for certain information needs.

5. "Data Collection Implementation" offers guidance in the ultimate choice of data collection methods and provides you with some tips and techniques for carrying out the data collection process.

6. "Data Analysis Findings" discusses your findings—what the data tells you about the training need being investigated. One of the most important points is the fact that findings are not the same thing as recommendations.

7. "Data Analysis Recommendations" demonstrates the difference between findings and recommendations. Recommendations are the needs assessor's actual conclusions and suggested actions that he or she thinks should be carried out. The needs assessor's role in identifying issues that are not related to training is also examined.

8. "Communicating With Your Client" presents communication techniques that can assist you in reaching your goal: the implementation of your recommendations. You will explore planning a presentation tailored to a specific client,

9. "The Ideal Organization Scan" goes beyond the real-world training needs assessment approach presented in this book. In the real world you often find yourself reacting to training requests. In a perfect world, you would have the time and resources to be proactive and engage your client by continuously scanning the organization and the external environment for information indicating trends and patterns in organization needs and training implications. Call it the Columbo approach, named after the famed TV detective who was always taking in and processing information to solve his cases.

10. "A Final Note" offers some food for thought about the role of training needs assessment in the organization and in the field of performance consulting. Ideas for further professional development are presented and a suggested reading list is provided with many sources to support your professional growth.

Icons to Guide You

This book employs icons that help you make optimal use of the information presented. You have already seen some of these icons used in this chapter.

What's Inside This Chapter

Each chapter opens with a short summary for your quick reference of what is in that chapter. You can use this section to identify the information in the chapter, and, if you wish, to skip ahead to the material that is most useful.

Basic Rule

These rules cut to the chase. They are unequivocal and important concepts in the area of training needs assessment.

Think About This

These are helpful tips that you can "put in your back pocket" to pull out when needed as you conduct a needs assessment.

Noted

This icon is used to give you more detail or explanation about a concept or a principle. Sometimes it is used for a short but productive tangent.

Getting It Done

The final section of each chapter supports your ability to take the content of that chapter and apply it. A progressive case study will be featured to challenge you in understanding and using the chapter content. Also, you will find tools that will assist you in applying the concepts to your own situation. Sometimes the tool is a list of questions for you to ponder, sometimes it is a self-assessment questionnaire, and sometimes it is a list of action steps you can take to enhance your training needs assessment skills.

Needs Assessment Basics will provide you with ample food for thought, tools, checklists, and worksheets to help you make these materials and concepts yours. Ready to get started? Chapter 2 will take you to the point in the needs assessment process where most training professionals find themselves—right in the middle!

2

The Training Request

What's Inside This Chapter

In this chapter, you'll learn:

▶ That training needs assessment usually begins "in the middle," with a training request from a client

▶ How to handle the initial client conversation about a training request

▶ What questions to ask a client to identify initial business needs, performance needs, learning needs, and learner needs

▶ Several different ways to handle the training request conversation so as to increase your credibility.

Starting in the Middle: The Training Request

You are walking down the hall in your organization minding your own business when you run into a department manager. You greet each other and chat for a moment and then the manager says, "You know, I'm having some trouble with my customer satisfaction measures in the call center. They seem to be in a decline. The phone representatives must not be as responsive to the customers as they should. Would you set up a telephone skills training session next Tuesday?"

Your first instinct would probably be to say, "Yes, certainly! What time?" but why? Among your choices:

A. You have an excellent telephone skills program that you have been wanting to pilot test, and this would be your chance to do so.
B. Part of the reason you chose the HRD field is because it is a helping profession that resonates for you, and this is an opportunity to help.
C. You are an excellent trainer, and this is a chance to shine.
D. You want to be responsive to your clients and build a reputation of responsiveness. After all, that's your job, isn't it?
E. This manager has a reputation for being demanding and no-nonsense—the only answer this manager is looking for is "yes," and that means a lot of pressure!

Most likely, you'd respond "All of the above." These issues exist for training professionals every time they have this conversation in the hall or when a manager asks them to stop by to talk about a training need. It's hard *not* to say yes immediately with these pressures.

Now look at the other side of the coin. What are some reasons that saying "Yes, certainly! What time?" would not be the best response?

A. You don't know how this problem (low customer satisfaction measures) fits into this manager's overall business strategy. (You could end up solving a problem that isn't very important.)
B. You don't know what the customer satisfaction numbers are or what they should be. (There is no business goal to focus on.)
C. You don't know what factors other than the phone representatives' job performance might be contributing to the decline in customer satisfaction measures. (It might not be a training problem at all.)
D. You don't know what the phone representatives are doing wrong. (You might not hit on the skills they need when you deliver your course.)
E. You don't know if the telephone skills course you have matches with what the representatives are doing wrong. (You might train them in skills they already know and miss the skills they need.)
F. You don't know how the phone representatives feel about their job performance or the prospect of participating in telephone skills training. (You

could insult them by teaching things they already know and thereby create or contribute to a morale issue.)

G. You don't know what kind of learning environment would be most conducive to the phone representatives' needs as learners. (You could end up delivering a course that's too easy, too challenging, too active, too inactive, too intimidating, or too uncomfortable and thereby impede their learning.)

If you again said "all of the above," you're on the right track. It can be difficult not to give a client an immediate yes, but the short-term gain obtained by being perceived as responsive by the client is outweighed by the long-term risk of not adding value and not impacting that client's business. Instead, it is time to have a training-need conversation with that client, and this chapter focuses on that part of the process. In this conversation, you will more than likely say "Yes, and . . ." rather than simply "yes."

Basic Rule 3

Many factors cause pressure to say an immediate "yes" to a training request. Resist the pressure.

Why Start Here?

Remember figure 1-2, which depicted the training needs assessment process? Here in figure 2-1 is the same diagram, with the topic for this chapter highlighted. You'll notice that the highlighted portion—the focus of this chapter—is the third step, not the first step, in the process. Why not start at the first step? Why start here?

This book starts here because this is where the process usually starts for most needs assessors—in the middle during the hallway conversation. What that means is that the first challenge for the needs assessor is to *step backward* in the process and place the training request in the context of the business needs. You must guide the conversation in the hallway (or more appropriately, in a scheduled meeting with adequate time allotted) away from identifying an intervention (where the client probably wants to go) to a more appropriate focus on the first two steps in the process:

1. Conduct external and organization scan.
2. Collect data to identify business needs.

Figure 2-1. The training needs assessment process with step 3 highlighted.

Step 1. Conduct external and organization scan

Step 2. Collect data to identify business needs

Capitalize on an opportunity
Resolve a problem
Support a strategy

Step 3. Identify potential training intervention

Step 4. Collect data to identify performance, learning, and learner needs

Required performance
Learners' current performance
Required skills and knowledge
Learners' current skills and knowledge
Learner needs

Step 5. Analyze data

Identify findings: gaps in performance, skills, and knowledge
Identify recommendations

Step 6. Deliver data analysis feedback

Training recommendations: design and delivery; ROI forecast
Non-training recommendations: work environment, rewards, consequences, work processes

Transition step: Begin training design

So, in essence, you have to redirect the conversation to focus on the first two steps because your client unknowingly entered the process at step 3. By focusing on the first two steps, you can express the training need in the context of the client's business needs.

Noted

Is there ever a time when the process actually begins as the beginning? Yes, it can. In fact, it is a worthy goal for training professionals to continuously scan the organization's internal and external business needs (steps 1 and 2) in order to identify potential training needs. In a perfect world, all training needs would be identified and explored in this manner (see chapter 9). For now, however, the focus is on how potential training needs are usually identified in the real world: The client initiates the training request.

The Initial Client Conversation

The initial conversation you conduct with your client provides some presenting indicators regarding the client's needs, setting you on the data collection trail (addressed in chapters 3, 4, and 5). Before starting down that trail, you must identify the business context. This conversation, therefore, has multiple goals:

- to identify the client's perceptions of the presenting need that has triggered the client to make the training request
- to place the presenting need in the context of the business by identifying the client's business needs and how the presenting need is linked to them
- to identify the client's perception of employee performance needs inherent in the situation
- to identify the client's perception of what the intended training intervention should address
- to identify the client's perception of the employees' needs as learning participants
- to set the stage for the possibility that there might be both training-related and non-training-related issues contributing to the presenting problem
- to gain permission and support for a needs assessment data collection effort to ensure the training will resolve the business and performance needs
- to establish a reasonable timeframe for the potential training deliverables.

Each set of information provides direction for your data collection efforts in the needs assessment process. Table 2-1 offers some questions that you can use during a client discussion to start identifying indicators for data collection. The questions are organized according to the needs assessment stages that were outlined in figure 1-1.

Basic Rule 4

In response to a training request, say "Yes—and here are the questions I must answer to fulfill your request."

Acting on a Hunch

Should you play out a hunch during this conversation? For example, what if a client says that training in a certain skill is needed for a group of employees, but your background and experience tell you that the desired training won't resolve the problem at hand? Your trainer's mind immediately forms an intuitive guess—a hunch—that there are other resolutions that will be more effective than the solution the client has chosen. Hunches are good things; they occur because you have seen patterns and trends and common cause-and-effect relationships during your experience in needs assessment and training. Many times—if not most times—your hunches are correct.

So, should you act on a hunch during this conversation? Should you present other possibilities to the client? Float a test balloon? Should you begin a line of questioning that takes the client off his or her path that a specific training solution is the answer? No, not yet. Although the client doesn't have any data at this point to prove his or her contention, neither do you. Postulating or speculating about solutions that represent disagreement with the client at this time only causes tension. Instead, negotiate to gather data regarding your hunch. When the time comes, the data will convince the client.

There are a couple other questions you may wish to ask during your initial conversation with the client. You could ask about the possibility of conducting a training needs assessment to collect more information regarding this training intervention. You could seize this opportunity to request access to data sources after you have identified them. Among the sources that your client should provide access to are organizational data collected in the client's department and in other departments (for example, customer service or the HR and quality improvement departments); managers of the

Table 2-1. Some questions to ask your client during an initial client discussion to trigger data collection.

Needs Assessment Stage	Questions
Stage 1: Business Needs	• What current business needs or strategies are being affected or perhaps caused by the presenting problem? • What business problems exist? (Look for such measures as amount of increase or decrease in business indicators, including waste, customer satisfaction, turnover, grievances, productivity, quality, complaints, and so forth. If actual measures are unknown by the client, this information is critical to find out during data collection.) • What is going on in the external environment that is related to this presenting problem (for example, competition, market changes, and government regulations)? • What other data exists (that your business unit already collects) that may provide information regarding this business need (sales, productivity, quality, HR information, benchmarking, and so forth)? • What change(s) in these business indicators are you seeking to achieve with this training intervention? What measures will tell you that you have been successful? • What business opportunities are inherent in this business need (for example, new markets or new products)? • What business strategy(ies) are you seeking to support with this requested training intervention? • What's happening in your business that shouldn't be happening? • What's not happening in your business that should be happening?
Stage 2: Performance Needs	• What results should employees be achieving? What is their current level of achievement? • What should people be doing differently? • What should they stop/start/keep doing? • What does perfect performance look like? What does current performance look like? • What else might be getting in the way of employees performing as they should, other than lack of skills and knowledge (non-training issues)? • What will be the nature of management support for job application and practice after training?
Stage 3: Learning Needs	• What knowledge and skills do you think the targeted employees need to learn to perform the way they should? • How important is each knowledge and skill that you have listed? • How well should they be performing the skills by the end of the training?
Stage 4: Learner Needs	• What are the targeted learners' backgrounds and experience in this subject matter? • What are their learning styles? • What is their job environment like (fast-paced, stressful, routine)? • What are the expectations regarding when and how they will attend the training (during work, after hours, paid, unpaid)?

targeted employees; the targeted employees themselves; aggregate performance appraisal data and trends on the targeted employees; exemplary employees; and subject matter experts.

Dealing With Non-Training Issues

One question listed in table 2-1 deals with non-training issues, which comprise such areas as lack of tools, equipment, resources; lack of policies or procedures to support the desired performance; ineffective or inefficient work processes; lack of management support for skill transfer back to the job after training; lack of incentives and rewards for producing desired performance; lack of negative consequences for undesirable performance; and lack of clear performance expectations. Some clients may not understand the question regarding non-training issues that might be getting in the way of performance, or they may be reluctant to answer. Others infer from this question that they are being accused of mistakenly choosing training as the solution for a problem. Others might not want to consider non-training issues because if a training issue has been identified, they have effectively transferred that problem to the training professional. Suggesting that there might be other causes that need to be addressed implies that the client—not the trainer—might have to deal with at least part of the problem. Once the client puts something on your plate, he or she really does not want any part of it handed back.

Think About This

Understanding and identifying performance issues involves a complex thought process. Robert Mager (1997a,b) of the Center for Effective Performance has developed a performance analysis thought process flowchart that is invaluable in helping sort out training and non-training issues.

Building Credibility

Will every client respond positively and collaboratively to the questioning suggested here? Not necessarily. Many organizations, and managers, view the training professional as a training provider—someone who simply delivers training as requested by the clients and has a limited role in the organization's performance issues. The first time you try to change this perception with a particular client by having a conversation about the needs underlying the training request, you might be met with surprise, impatience, or annoyance.

What is depicted in this picture? If you said an egg, you're right. And, if you said a chicken, you're right. Which came first? Right again!

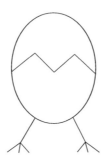

Some days you will choose to be the chicken, and some days you will choose to be the egg. In other words, there will be times when you ask for and will be given credibility and permission for your needs assessment effort through your client's giving you the benefit of the doubt and accepting your questions and approach. With this client, you simply enhance (and earn) the credibility that has already been bestowed by conducting a thorough and effective training needs assessment.

There will be other times as well, when a client forces you to prove that your approach works—no giving the benefit of the doubt here! You will simply say yes to a perceived training need and then find ways to build aspects of the needs assessment into the delivery of the training. At the end of the project, you can then build credibility with this client by saying, "I also did some needs assessment work during the training delivery, and here is what I found out about what is affecting the performance that you require." The additional information is right on target and allows you to begin building credibility with that client.

Why do it one way with one client and another way with a different client? Client perceptions regarding internal training professionals vary according to organizational culture, past history with other training professionals, past history with you, perceptions of training that are individual to each client, and understanding of the HRD field. What works with one client will not work with another. If the needs assessor doesn't vary the approach according to the client's characteristics in this initial conversation, opportunities for impact will be lost. The ultimate paradox is that if you don't adjust your approach to focus on building credibility in a way that works in the situation, credibility will never be established.

Must you always fulfill a client's training request? How can you maintain your credibility if your hunches and the data and your background and your experience all indicate that the issue is not a skill deficiency and, therefore, not a training issue? Will you still have to deliver a training solution? Sometimes yes, sometimes no.

If you have been permitted to conduct a needs assessment, it appears that the client is at least somewhat willing to explore other possibilities. Once you have gathered and analyzed your data and the indicators are clear, these clients are willing to be convinced, especially if you have good recommendations regarding the non-training issues you have identified (and if you still deliver some type of training intervention as part of the solution).

Other clients are so determined that the solution is a training intervention that they cannot be convinced otherwise—at least not until the training is delivered and the evidence that it was not a training issue is irrefutable. With these clients, conducting a needs assessment is difficult, if not impossible. Sometimes the best answer is something like: "Yes, I can deliver the telephone skills training next Tuesday, *and* I would like to use some of the session to gather information about what else might be contributing to the decline in customer satisfaction figures." Then you deliver both the training and the value-added needs assessment activities that you propose. This tactic might not secure permission for your needs assessment on this project, but it will build credibility for the next interaction with that client.

So—be the chicken one day, and be the egg another day. Do what works to achieve your ultimate goal: conducting a thorough, effective training needs assessment.

Getting It Done

How you handle the initial conversation with a potential client about a potential training intervention is critical in shaping how you will deliver your services to that client and how useful your services will be to that client's business goals. This initial conversation also influences your future relationship with that client and your credibility as a training professional. The following two exercises (exercises 2-1 and 2-2) will help you begin to think about your role as a needs assessor in your organization, and in relation to a specific client you might work with.

Exercise 2-1. Importance assessment.

Circle the response below (low, medium, high) that indicates the importance of each training needs assessment purpose as it applies to your organization. Take note of the items that you mark high and jot some notes in the rightmost column to help you prepare to explain those items to your client or manager when called upon to do so.

Purpose of Training Needs Assessment	Importance in My Organization			Explanation
Placing a client's stated training need or request in the context of the organization's needs	Low	Medium	High	
Validating and augmenting the initial issues presented by the client	Low	Medium	High	
Ensuring that the ultimate training design will support employee performance and thereby help the organization meet its needs	Low	Medium	High	
Identifying recommendations regarding non-training issues that are affecting the achievement of the desired organization and employee performance goals	Low	Medium	High	
Ensuring survival of the training function	Low	Medium	High	
Establishing the foundation for back-end evaluation	Low	Medium	High	

Exercise 2-2. Preparing for the initial client conversation.

Think about a current client with whom you work. Imagine that this client has asked you into his or her office and has requested a training program.

Now, consider these questions:

1. What is this client's current perception of what training and HRD professionals do?

   _____

2. What is this client's perception of the role of training in supporting business strategies and employee performance?

   _____

(continued on page 24)

Exercise 2-2. Preparing for the initial client conversation (continued).

3. What questions will you ask this client in order to (a) place the training request in the context of business and performance needs; and (b) build credibility in order to conduct a training needs assessment?

    _____

    _____

    _____

As mentioned in chapter 1, a progressive case study is featured in this book to challenge you in understanding and using the chapter content in a situation similar to one you might find in your organization. In exercise 2-3, a step in the case needs assessment process is described, and you are asked to identify or discuss what Chris, the training professional in the case, should do next. A potential answer is presented in the following chapter to guide you in evaluating your response.

Exercise 2-3. The Whitewater Outfitters case study (part 1).

Whitewater Outfitters (a fictitious company) is an apparel manufacturing and retail company specializing in upscale outdoor sportswear. The company supports multiple manufacturing plants in various sections of the country. The plants are considered to be silos; that is, each plant produces only certain specific lines of sportswear. Additional operations include retail stores in outdoor resort areas of the country and a very busy catalog sales business.

Manufacturing production in the plants is accomplished through production teams. Each team has a leader who coordinates and assigns work. The team leaders run their production lines and are responsible for hiring, training, and performance management of their teams. All team members are cross-trained so that each member of a team can run any part of that production line.

Chris Martin is a training professional in the Davidson City plant. Chris is quite excited, as is the rest of the plant, about a recent announcement. Whitewater has announced in the press the addition of a brand new line of sportswear, called the City Slicker line. The new line will include men's, women's, and children's summer and winter apparel, shoes and boots, coats, and accessories. Much of the new line will be manufactured in the Davidson City plant.

Chris has been asked to come to a meeting with the plant production manager L.K. Stewart to discuss an upcoming training need. After greeting each other and settling in at the conference table, Stewart shares with Chris some of the specifics regarding establishing production of the City Slicker line in the plant:

- The City Slicker line of clothing and accessories will be supported by three new production lines scheduled to start up in six months.
- Some of the operations will be similar to those already in place in the plant, and a few will be new processes.
- The new lines will require hiring 50 new employees. Some of the new employees will be assigned to the City Slicker line teams, and others will be assigned to existing line teams. Some current employees will move to City Slicker line teams, and others will remain on current line teams.
- The hiring push for the 50 new employees will begin in three months.

L.K. concludes, "So you see, Chris, all the team leaders will be interviewing and hiring team members. We need to make sure we get excellent workers, not like some of the problem employees we've had lately. I want you to design and teach a job interviewing skills class for the team leaders, and I want you to do it by the time the hiring push begins."

How should Chris handle the rest of this conversation? What questions should Chris ask Stewart? Write down your suggested questions here:

_____

_____

_____

_____

The main purpose of the initial conversation is to gain permission to conduct a needs assessment, which places a training request within the context of the organization's business needs and the client's business needs, and anchors the eventual training to the job performance that will be required to meet the business needs. Now that this permission has been obtained, it is time to plan the data collection for the needs assessment study.

3

Identifying Questions
and Data Sources

What's Inside This Chapter

In this chapter, you'll learn:

▶ The purposes of training needs assessment data collection
▶ Why developing data collection questions, identifying data sources, identifying potential data collection methods, and choosing data collection methods should constitute four distinct thought processes
▶ Common data collection questions
▶ Characteristics of data sources.

The Purposes of Training Needs Assessment Data Collection and Analysis

Training interventions are designed to help employee-learners master knowledge and skills, which in turn support their increased job performance, which in turn supports the business goals linked to that performance. Training needs assessment is the foundation that guarantees the eventual training design and delivery hit the mark—at all four needs assessment stages (see figure 1-1).

You will notice in figure 3-1 that this chapter addresses the fourth step in the training needs assessment process. This is the point at which you collect data at needs assessment stages 2, 3, and 4 (performance needs, learning needs, and learner needs, respectively) to establish the need for training. Remember also that the common scenario presented in this book assumes that you have entered the process in the middle; that is, at the point where a potential training intervention has been identified at step 3. Because of that, your data collection process must also take a step back so you can gather data to identify business needs as well, for steps 1 and 2. (Chapter 9 addresses following the needs assessment phases in the "right" order.)

Training needs assessment data collection serves multiple purposes:

- augments and validates the client's presenting business needs
- links the business needs to the client's goal and the desired training intervention
- validates or refutes the hunches that came to you during the initial client conversation
- defines the business gap between the current business needs and the desired business goals
- defines the performance gap between the current learner performance level and the desired learner performance level
- defines the knowledge/skill gap between the desired learner skills/knowledge level and the desired skills/knowledge level
- identifies learners' needs in the learning environment (the conditions that exist in the classroom, lab, or other area where learning takes place).

Identifying the gap between actual and desired performance at each stage is critical to ensure that the eventual training design is tailored to bridge the gaps. Training

Think About This

By now you've noticed that the terms "employee" and "learner" seem to be used almost interchangeably. Actually, there is a pattern: When the employees who are to be training participants are referred to in the organizational or business context, the term "employees" is used. When they are referred to in the training or learning context, the term "learners" is used.

Figure 3-1. The training needs assessment process with step 4 highlighted.

Step 1. Conduct external and organization scan

Step 2. Collect data to identify business needs

Capitalize on an opportunity
Resolve a problem
Support a strategy

Step 3. Identify potential training intervention

Step 4. Collect data to identify performance, learning, and learner needs

Required performance
Learners' current performance
Required skills and knowledge
Learners' current skills and knowledge
Learner needs

Step 5. Analyze data

Identify findings: gaps in performance, skills, and knowledge
Identify recommendations

Step 6. Deliver data analysis feedback

Training recommendations: design and delivery; ROI forecast
Non-training recommendations: work environment, rewards, consequences, work processes

Transition step: Begin training design

that is designed to bridge performance and learning gaps adds value and, ultimately, impacts the business in a positive direction.

Noted

If a training request is geared toward learners who have no background or experience in the skills, measuring the gap by comparing current performance to desired performance is not necessary. Current performance is assumed to be zero, so data needs to be collected only on desired performance.

Four Distinct Thought Processes

Planning your data collection consists of four separate thought processes:

1. identifying the questions that must be answered by the data collection
2. identifying the sources that can supply the required data
3. identifying potential data collection methods
4. choosing the data collection methods.

Why is it important to keep these thought processes and decisions separate? Too often a needs assessor says, "I will interview so-and-so" or "I will conduct a focus group with these employees" and so on. In essence, the four thought processes—the question, source, potential method, and ultimate method—have been collapsed into one thought process, which results in the premature identification of the data collection method to be used.

When you jump to identify a method too quickly, you have closed down the creative thinking that is necessary for good data collection. What if, for whatever reason, that particular individual can't be interviewed, or those people aren't available for a focus group? Because the question, data source, potential data collection methods, and ultimate data collection method were decided together, all four decisions become foregone conclusions. When one of those decisions cannot be implemented, the other three collapse with it. Whether you call it data collection tunnel vision, jumping to conclusions, narrowing the process too soon, or even thinking inside the box, it's very difficult to regroup and think about alternative methods. Because the initial thinking was unnecessarily limited by the realities inherent in actually collecting the data, there is a distinct possibility of missing key questions and data sources in the earlier thought processes.

The initial thinking (identifying questions, data sources, and potential data collection methods) should not be limited by reality. Instead, keep the first three thought processes open. If you could ask any questions that you wanted, what would they be? What would be your data sources if there were no constraints? When you get to the fourth decision, choosing data collection methods (chapter 5), there is time enough to ground the data collection process in the limits of reality. Those limits will include time, cost, access to information, geography, available technology, and value of the data to the project. You will end up picking and choosing data collection methods that will gain you the most data and the most useful data with a minimum expenditure of resources.

Basic Rule 5

Identifying data collection questions, identifying data sources, identifying potential data collection methods, and choosing data collection methods are four distinct tasks and thought processes.

Some trainers want to collect all of the data that could possibly pertain to the training issue at hand. They become enamored of the data collection process because research is interesting to them. Research is all well and good; however, the purpose of needs assessment data collection is not research. It is to help the client "mobilize action on a problem" (Block, 2000). This aspect is what makes training needs assessment different from research. The main objective of data collection in training needs assessment is "action, not understanding" (Block, 2000). By breaking down the choice of a data collection method into distinct thought processes, the result is a narrowing-down process that culminates in the selection of the best, most effective, and most efficient data collection methods for the needs assessment project at hand.

The Data Collection Plan

Figure 3-2 presents a tool that is useful for organizing your data collection and for keeping your four thought processes separate. The second column in the plan is

Figure 3-2. Data collection plan.

DATA COLLECTION PLAN

PROJECT: _____

Needs Assessment Stage	Questions to Be Answered	Data Sources	Potential Data Collection Method(s)	Data Collection Method
Stage 1: Business Needs				
Stage 2: Performance Needs				
Stage 3: Learning Needs				
Stage 4: Learner Needs				

intended for you to insert your data collection questions; in the next column, you will insert a potential data source for each question. In the fourth column are listed all of the potential data collection methods that could be used to address the question and access the source, and in the final column the ultimate data collection method decision is listed. In this chapter, you will work on completing the second and third columns. You will then complete the plan in the next chapters.

The data collection plan is a tool for you, not your client. When the plan is completed, you can transform the last column—the ultimate data collection method decision—into a proposal or memo for your client requesting permission to implement the methods and the necessary access. The plan then becomes your roadmap for implementing data collection. Later, it can also serve as part of the outline for your presentation of findings and recommendations.

Data Collection Questions

Based on your initial conversation with your client, you must develop data collection questions. What do you want to know at each stage—business needs, performance needs, learning needs, and learner needs? Table 3-1 presents some examples of targeted questions for each needs assessment stage that can be customized to a specific data collection plan.

Identifying Data Sources

Now that you have developed some data collection questions, a data source must be identified for each question. Remember, this is not about identifying the data collection *method* (for example, a focus group); it is about identifying the data *source* (for example, a specific group of people). This can be a tough distinction to make, so it can take some work to think about the data source apart from the data collection method.

Table 3-2 provides a list of potential data sources, the type of data that the source usually provides (by needs assessment stage), and comments regarding advantages and disadvantages of the particular data sources.

It is now clear that some data sources can provide data at multiple stages of needs assessment. When data collection is designed and implemented, the methods must be carefully designed to cover all data needs in one collection effort. No data source wants to be contacted multiple times just to be asked a few different questions each time!

Table 3-1. Examples of data collection questions.

Needs Assessment Stage	Example Questions
Stage 1: Business Needs	• What problem(s) must be resolved? To what measurable extent? • What opportunity(ies) must be capitalized upon? What is the initial goal? • What strategy(ies) must be supported? What measures will indicate success? • What proportion of the problem, opportunity, or strategic goal will be attributed to the training effort?
Stage 2: Performance Needs	• What is a description of desired on-the-job performance? • What is a description of current on-the-job performance? • What are the specific gaps between desired and current on-the-job performance? • How is on-the-job performance measured? • How is on-the-job-performance managed and rewarded? • What tools and resources do the employees need to achieve the desired performance? • What is a description of the work environment in which the performance is expected? • What are posttraining expectations for manager support for job application?
Stage 3: Learning Needs	• What do learners know now? • What can learners do now? • What do the learners need to be able to *do* (skills) differently? How well? • What do learners need to know to do (perform the skills)? • What are implications in the work environment for transfer of learning back to the job?
Stage 4: Learner Needs	• What training have the learners already had in this area? • How did previous training go? • What are their learning styles? • What is their attitude about the job performance that is being targeted? • What is their attitude toward the planned training program? • What organizational levels will the learners come from? • What will be the context in which they attend training (on the job, off the job; before or after shift; with their managers' support or not; arrangements made to be away from work, or expected to catch up on work during breaks)? • Will training attendance be voluntary or mandatory?

Table 3-2. Data sources for training needs assessment.

Data Source	Type of Data and Needs Assessment Stage	Advantages of Source	Disadvantages of Source
Extant[1] data: Annual reports, benchmarking studies, sales figures, complaints, quality, customer satisfaction, productivity, HR data	Business needs information (stage 1)	Data has already been collected and is easy to obtain; may need your client to provide an entrée to the data source	Data was not collected for your purpose; must extrapolate from the data to find indicators of the information you need
Upper management/client	Business needs information (stage 1)	Excellent source regarding priorities of the business and what is really important	Access may be limited or even non-existent as you go higher in the organization
Learners' managers	Desired performance (stage 2) Current performance (stage 2)	Can speak very clearly to the results learners are to achieve on the job and to expected on-the-job behaviors	Not necessarily cognizant of non-training issues inherent in the work environment; sometimes will try to dictate what the learning should look like; must keep managers on track to address performance only
Subject matter experts (internal or external, or resource materials)	Desired performance (stage 2) Desired knowledge and skills (stage 3)	Gives a clear picture of what performance looks like and what knowledge and skills it takes to get that performance	Cannot necessarily translate expertise into learning terms; training professional must be able to do that
Extant data: job descriptions, performance evaluation data[2], 360-degree aggregate data	Current performance (stage 2)	Data has already been collected and is easy to obtain; may need your client to provide an entrée to the data source	Data was not collected for your purpose; must extrapolate from the data to find indicators of the information needed

[1] Data that already exists in the organization or external to the organization.
[2] Data is needed only in aggregate form because the goal is to identify performance of a group; individual data is neither necessary nor desirable.

(continued on page 36)

Table 3-2. Data sources for training needs assessment (continued).

Data Source	Type of Data and Needs Assessment Stage	Advantages of Source	Disadvantages of Source
Star performers	Desired performance (stage 2)	Is the best source of information on what excellent performance looks like because they do it every day	Performance may be so second nature that they can't identify components; needs assessor must do that
Customers	Desired performance (stage 2) Current performance (stage 2)	Gives clear picture of what customers want, which is a key performance driver; and gives clear picture of what they are getting and their level of satisfaction.	Customer feedback is without organization context of performance expectations, logistics, and feasibility of doing what they want
Learners	Current performance (stage 2) Learning needs (stage 3) Learner needs (stage 4)	Provides a great deal of information at multiple levels: what they do now, what they need to learn, how they need to learn	Sometimes uncomfortable with giving information and may give distorted data
Other training professionals	Learning needs (stage 3) Learner needs (stage 4)	Other trainers who have trained the target group can give information about skill levels and what learners need to learn, as well as on techniques and activities that work or don't work	Hard to tell how much of their feedback is influenced by their own training methods or other biases
Extant data: Previous training evaluation information	Learning needs (stage 3) Learner needs (stage 4)	Gives information in learners' own perceptions regarding their learning needs and what works for them in the learning environment	Depth of information depends on context of when learners filled out training evaluations; if it was in the last five minutes of a previous training course, the data won't have much meaning

36

Getting It Done

There are multiple challenges inherent in planning data collection for a needs assessment study. You must obtain permission from your client to gain access to data sources, and your client must sometimes obtain that access for you. You must identify the most critical questions to be answered, and you must ascertain how much data gathering will provide the needed data. Nevertheless, it is important to remember that this is not a research study—it is a study regarding actions that must be taken.

Now, it's time to look in on Chris Martin to see how things are going at Whitewater Outfitters. Help Chris with step 4 of the needs assessment process by completing the first two columns of the data collection plan provided in exercise 3-1.

Exercise 3-1. The Whitewater Outfitter case study (part 2).

In the meeting with L.K. Stewart, Chris Martin asked targeted questions of this client to get a clearer picture of the context surrounding the need for interview skills training for the team leaders. In table 3-1, you were introduced to some of the questions that Chris asked.

When asked about business needs, Stewart shared the following:

- The team leaders must be ready to conduct interviews and begin hiring in three months.
- This plant's teams have an employee turnover rate that is 12 percent higher than the industry average. Stewart has heard through the grapevine that the employees who are leaving are going to jobs at Eddie Bean, another sportswear company plant on the other side of town.
- Complaints from retail store personnel and mail-order customers regarding poor quality merchandise in existing product lines from this plant are currently at an all-time high, indicating there are production issues on the current lines.
- There have been four Equal Employment Opportunity (EEO) complaints from the production teams this fiscal year.

Not only does Stewart want the team leaders ready for the hiring push in three months, there are other expectations that must be met in six months after the new lines are up and running: lower turnover rates within the teams; fewer complaints about poor quality from the retail stores and mail-order customers; and zero EEO complaints initiated by the teams.

When asked about performance needs, Stewart's responses are:

- All of the team leaders will have to interview and hire new team members from both internal and external sources because all teams will lose some members to the new production lines.

Exercise 3-1. The Whitewater Outfitter case study (part 2).

- The team leaders as a group have poor interviewing skills. Poor interviewing skills lead to mismatched hiring decisions. Mismatched new hires leave quickly. If they are under-qualified for the job, they quit due to frustration and stress; if overqualified, they quit due to boredom. Therefore, mismatched hiring decisions directly affect the high turnover that the plant is experiencing. Mismatched new hires also lead to quality complaints because employees who are not a good match for their jobs produce low-quality products.
- Stewart believes that the team leaders are asking illegal interview questions that result in EEO-related issues and expose the plant and Whitewater Outfitters to legal liability issues and potential lawsuits.

Stewart sees the learning needs (the skills the team leaders must perform better on) as

- preparing for an interview
- conducting an interview
- asking legal interview questions
- making sound hiring decisions that lead to hiring people who are good matches with the job and job environment in the plant.

Stewart shared the following information about the team leaders as learners:

- The team leaders have never had any training on job interviewing skills in this plant. Therefore, whatever they are doing (right or wrong), they learned on their own.

By the end of the conversation, Stewart had offered to pave the way by sending intro-ductory emails and, in the case of the team leaders, allowing time for Chris to have access to the following people for data collection:

- Tracy Waddell, director of human resources
- Syd Diaz and Morgan Ciscyk, team leaders
- Riley Johnson, manager of the complaint center.

Chris knows that data collection involves augmenting and validating the client's present-ing issues as well as collecting additional data at all four needs assessment stages. What questions should Chris seek to answer in the data collection process? And, what data sources will answer these questions? Complete the second two columns of Chris's data collection plan ("Questions to be Answered" and "Data Source"). Don't list data collection methods yet; you'll have a chance to do that in the next chapter.

DATA COLLECTION PLAN

PROJECT: Interviewing Skills for Team Leaders, Davidson City Plant, Whitewater Outfitters

Needs Assessment Stage	Questions to Be Answered	Data Source	Potential Data Collection Method(s)	Data Collection Method
Stage 1: Business Needs				
Stage 2: Performance Needs				
Stage 3: Learning Needs				
Stage 4: Learner Needs				

OK, you helped Chris begin a data collection plan for the needs assessment at Whitewater Outfitters. Now, think about a training needs assessment project that *you* are working on right now, or one that you know you will be working on in the future. Make a photocopy of figure 3-2, which is a tool for you to list your data collection questions and your data sources. Don't list potential data collection methods yet; that will be your job in the next chapter.

It may appear that step 4 in the needs assessment process is complete now that you have reached the end of this chapter. In truth, step 4 continues in chapters 4 and 5.

4

Evaluating Potential Data Collection Methods

What's Inside This Chapter

In this chapter, you'll learn:

▶ How step 4 in the needs assessment process continues with the collection of relevant data
▶ The difference between quantitative and qualitative data collection measures
▶ How and when to apply different types of analytical approaches for common data collection methods.

Understanding Data Collection Methods

This chapter continues step 4 in the training needs assessment process (see figure 3-1). In chapter 3, you examined the four distinct thought processes inherent in data collection, and you developed your data collection plan. In this chapter, data collection methods are analyzed for their uses, strengths, and weaknesses so that potential methods for each data source can be identified. With that information in hand, you will be able to choose the optimal methods to implement for your situation.

Data collection methods are either qualitative or quantitative. Quantitative methods are those that result in what is called hard data. Hard data is objective and measurable, whether stated in terms of frequency, percentage, proportion, or time. Qualitative measures yield soft data. These types of measures are more intangible, anecdotal, personal, and subjective, as in opinions, attitudes, assumptions, feelings, values, and desires. Qualitative data cannot be objectified, and that is the characteristic that makes the data valuable. For example, knowing how job performers feel (qualitative measure) about a skill will be just as important in the ultimate training design as knowing how well (quantitative measure) they perform it.

Noted

It is beyond the scope of this book to provide detailed instructions for implementing all potential needs assessment data collection methods. What is provided here are explanations of the most frequently used methods and the basic how-to's. References to other sources for data collection are provided in the Additional Resources and References sections at the back of this book. Zemke and Kramlinger's (1982) book (a classic in the HRD field) provides very detailed and helpful information regarding how to implement specific (particularly quantitative) data collection methods.

Quantitative and qualitative measures can be combined in a data collection process for excellent results. For example, you can use a qualitative method (say, interviews) to collect anecdotes and examples. Then you can develop a quantitative method (say, a survey) using the collected anecdotes and examples as survey items and measure how many respondents fit the examples and how frequently the examples fit the respondents. Conversely, a quantitative method can be used first to collect information on frequency and number of respondents. Then a qualitative method can be used to flesh out the survey items with richer detail. Qualitative and quantitative measures can also be combined in the same measurement tool. For example, items on a survey can be qualitative items, such as feelings or opinions. How many times each item is chosen (frequency) is a quantitative measure.

Quantitative Data Collection Methods

Extant Data. Existing records, reports, and data comprise extant data, which may be available inside the organization or external to it. Examples include job descriptions,

Basic Rule 6

Both quantitative and qualitative data collection methods add value to the needs assessment process.

competency models, benchmarking reports, annual reports, financial statements, strategic plans, mission statements, staffing statistics, climate surveys, 360-degree feedback, performance appraisals, grievances, turnover rates, absenteeism, suggestion box feedback, accident statistics, short-term and long-term leave records, customer complaints, quality statistics, production and labor costs, production rates, waste, rework rates, down time, late deliveries, repairs, training evaluation data, and competitive intelligence.

Extant data is often used for stage 1 and 2 measures for training needs assessment (business needs analysis and current performance analysis). Table 4-1 lists some advantages and disadvantages of using extant data for training needs assessment.

Table 4-1. Advantages and disadvantages of using extant data for training needs assessments.

Advantages	Disadvantages
• Hard data and measures • Can examine trends and patterns in the data over time • Consistent measurements provide reliable data • Does not involve individual employee confidentiality issues because data is used in aggregate form	• Usually collected for purposes other than training needs assessment, so training issues must be inferred from patterns in the data • No control over the methodology that was used to collect the data • Can be mixed in with data that is extraneous to your purpose so it must be "sifted"

Several methods are commonly used for collecting extant data. You can contact internal departments—HR, quality improvement, legal, finance, and so forth—that might have collected information that applies to the training need. Your client may have to pave the way by making the request for you. You can also proactively scan the external environment by keeping up with business trends, company progress, regulatory issues, and current events. (Organization scans are discussed more fully in chapter 9.)

Basic Rule 7

Information that will be useful in your situation and to your needs assessment purpose must usually be inferred from extant data.

Surveys. These are paper/pencil or electronic/email questionnaires that ask respondents a series of focused questions. Table 4-2 lists some advantages and disadvantages of using survey instruments for training needs assessment. Surveys are most often used for stages 2 and 4 measures for training needs assessment (performance analysis and learner analysis).

Table 4-2. Advantages and disadvantages of surveys for training needs assessments.

Advantages	Disadvantages
• Inexpensive • Results are easy to tally • Easy for respondents to participate • Gets quick results • Frequencies (how many respondents answered a question each way) are easy to understand • Can be qualitative also: Soft data questions yield qualitative data; the answer tally is quantitative	• It is challenging to construct questions that get the desired data in a configuration that meets your needs (must be careful with wording) • It is necessary to ensure that the wording of a question means the same thing to all respondents (reliability) and that the wording of the question will garner the information that is sought (face validity) • Choosing an appropriate answer scale is critical • Respondents can skew the results by simply checking all one type of answer without really reading the questions • Sometimes can't get a large enough sample to make the data reliable

When implementing surveys, it is important to formulate questions carefully to make sure they are clear as to interpretation. It's a good idea to pilot a survey with a small sample of the audience population to ensure that the items are unambiguous and that the survey has face validity and reliability.

Types of survey questions include yes/no, checklist, scaled (for example, on a Likert scale), and open-ended (completion of statements). You can even combine two rating scales for cross-referencing of data. Figure 4-1 is an example of a survey using two scales in this way.

Figure 4-1. Example of using two ranking scales on a survey instrument.

INSTRUCTIONAL STRATEGIES NEEDS ANALYSIS
For potential participants in train-the-trainer course

Please rank the following items twice on a scale of 1–5. The first ranking is the *importance* of this item to you, based on your job responsibilities (1 = not important at all, 5 = critical). The second ranking is a *self-assessment regarding your level of knowledge* (1 = I don't know very much about this subject, 5 = I am expert in this subject).

Item	Importance (1–5)	Self-Ranking (1–5)
The experiential learning process and discovery learning		
Designing lectures		
Facilitating lectures		
Designing structured exercises		
Facilitating structured exercises		
Designing case studies		
Facilitating case studies		
Designing role plays		
Facilitating role plays		
Designing demonstration/practices		
Facilitating demonstration/practices		
Other types of learning activities (please write in)		
Setting up learning activities: grouping and instructions		
Designing activity debriefs		
Facilitating activity debriefs		
Adjusting facilitation on the fly to compensate for time, experience levels, hot issues, glitches		
Personalizing facilitation with stories, analogies, puzzles, and so forth		
Choosing media (flipcharts, overheads, handouts, computer, video)		
Designing media		
Facilitating with media		
Developing facilitator guides		

Basic Rule 8

Pilot test a survey with a sample of the intended population to ensure reliability in the meaning of the questions.

Think About This

Some professionals call it "statistics" and some call it "sadistics"—you make the call! Although more discussion of statistics is included in chapter 6, the terms "reliability" and "validity" have already been used here, so short definitions will be useful. In essence, reliability and validity are parameters that indicate whether a data collection method actually measures what it is supposed to measure. Specifically, a question or survey item is deemed reliable if it means the same thing to every respondent who answers the question and that the same respondents answer the question the same way if it is presented to them multiple times. Face validity means that the question appears to ask what it is intended to ask and it appears to be related to the needs assessment at hand. Construct validity means that the question accurately obtains the information that is sought. This is the purpose behind pilot testing a data collection method (say, a survey) with a small sample—to ensure reliability and validity of the resulting data.

Assessments and Tests. These instruments gauge what the respondents know, can do, or believe in relation to the training need being investigated. Types of assessments include

- knowledge assessments through verbal or written responses to multiple choice, true/false, fill-in-the-blank, or essay questions
- actual performance of a job skill while being observed
- analysis of work results, product, or output against quality criteria.

Assessments and tests are most often used for stages 2 and 3 measures for training needs assessment to gauge current learner knowledge, skill, or performance levels. Table 4-3 identifies some advantages and disadvantages of using tests and assessments for training needs analysis.

Table 4-3. Advantages and disadvantages of tests/assessments for training needs analysis.

Advantages	Disadvantages
• Objective • Specifically identifies gap between current and desired performance, knowledge, and skills • Ultimate training design focuses on the specific gap rather than on generalized information	• Assessments don't always get to the thought processes behind why a participant performed in a certain way; accompanying with an interview can yield more complete data • Some participants can "freeze" and perform poorly due to test anxiety • Sometimes can be challenging to include both knowledge and skill tests/assessments due to time constraints in the training

It is critical to formulate questions and measurement criteria carefully to make sure they are clear as to interpretation when constructing a test. Consider using an expert in test writing to ensure validity beyond pilot testing if the content is highly technical or if you will be limited in using other methods to corroborate the needs assessment outcome. And, as is true with surveys, you should pilot the assessment with a small sample of the population to ensure face validity and reliability.

Basic Rule 9

Use a test-writing expert if assessments or tests are on highly technical subjects or if a test or assessment will be the sole, or one of very few, methods used.

Noted

The term "assessment" can also refer to instruments that measure frequency of behaviors, for example, a 360-degree feedback assessment or a commercially produced assessment of leadership behaviors used in conjunction with a model of leadership behavior. Such assessments can be produced internally or provided by external suppliers. The key is making sure that the assessment results provide information that will be useful in meeting the training need. Assessments can be used to gather others' perceptions of the targeted learners' behaviors or the learners' self-assessments of their own behaviors.

Job Task Analysis. This type of data collection involves a detailed examination (usually by interview and observation of a subject matter expert) of what it takes to do a job task, step by step. Job task analysis is most often used for analysis of desired performance (stages 2 and 3 measures). Some of the advantages and disadvantages of this data collection method are highlighted in table 4-4.

Table 4-4. Advantages and disadvantages of job task analysis for training needs assessments.

Advantages	Disadvantages
• Best input into training design: provides content and materials that will translate into rich detail for learning activities that replicate the job environment and serve as a basis for skill and knowledge testing in the ultimate training course • Standards of performance included in the task analysis can be quantitative as well	• Subject matter expert who is the data source must be seen as accurate and credible in the eyes of the organization • Time consuming for the needs assessor to interview and observe the subject matter expert

Through careful interview with, and observation of the subject matter expert, the needs assessor identifies and documents the following:

1. the task
2. the steps to complete the task
3. performance standards (sometimes one standard for the entire task and sometimes several standards for each step)
4. supporting task steps, knowledge, and attitudes necessary for successful task completion (eventually translated into enabling learning objectives during training design)
5. resources necessary to complete the task
6. description of the job environment
7. job performance objective—a statement depicting what the task looks like on the job—which is eventually translated into a terminal learning objective in the training design process.

There are several methodologies for conducting task analyses. Figures 4-2 and 4-3 present two simple examples of job task analysis. Figure 4-2 is a task analysis for an *intellectual* skill ("develop legal interview questions"), and figure 4-3 is for a *physical* skill ("hang a shower curtain"). Although hanging a shower curtain may seem a little silly as a task analysis, it is important that these examples represent skills that you are presumably familiar with so that you can see how steps and standards of familiar content are illustrated. If the content of the task analysis were unfamiliar skills to you, you could miss the linkages that are illustrated between steps and standards.

Note that in figure 4-2, there are performance standards for key task steps; in figure 4-3, the performance standard refers to the entire task.

Figure 4-2. Example of a job task analysis for an intellectual task/skill.

JOB TASK ANALYSIS: Interviewing Skills Course

Job Task/Skill: *Develop legal interview questions.*

Task Steps:

1. Analyze job description and résumé and identify areas that should be examined in the job interview.
2. Make a list of specific items that should each have a specific interview question.
3. Draft an interview question for each item.
4. Assess each question for job-relatedness and absence of illegal references.
5. Revise questions where applicable.
   - Standard: All questions are job related and contain no illegal references.

Supporting Knowledge:

- Review considerations in analyzing résumés.
- List the steps in the thought process that support the creation of legal, job-related questions.
- Describe EEO requirements that affect how organizations conduct job interviews.
- Differentiate between legal and illegal questions.

Supporting Attitude:

- Commit to preparing interview questions before the interview.
- Advocate developing questions that are both legal and job related.

Resources:

- Job description
- Job applicant's résumé

Job Environment Description:

The environment is a stressful and rushed one in which it is difficult for learners to find quiet time to prepare for interviews. Consequently, they are tempted to wing it and form questions during the interview itself rather than beforehand, which results in a higher likelihood of illegal questions being used. Pressure exists to do this task correctly in light of previous legal problems.

JOB PERFORMANCE OBJECTIVE:

Given a job description and an applicant's résumé, develop interview questions that are job related and contain no illegal references.

Figure 4-3. Example of a job task analysis for a physical task/skill.

JOB TASK ANALYSIS: <u>Training Course on Bathroom Decorating</u>

<u>Job Task/Skill:</u> *Hang a new shower curtain.*

<u>Job Task Steps:</u>

1. Take the new curtain out of the plastic cover.
2. Shake the curtain out.
   - ◆ Standard: Fold lines/wrinkles begin to disappear.
3. Open the package of plastic hangers.
4. Place the "hook" of the first hanger in the "hole" at one end of the top of the shower curtain.
   - ◆ Standard: Little plastic "filler dot" in shower curtain hole has been removed.
5. Hang the curved part of the first hanger on the shower rod (use a stool to reach the rod if necessary).
   - ◆ Standard: The shower curtain design is facing out into the bathroom.
6. Repeat steps 4 and 5 until all the hangers are on the rod and the curtain is hanging.
   - ◆ Standard: The curtain is spread out over the length of the curtain rod.
7. Clean up all the little "filler dots" that have fallen into the bathtub.
   - ◆ Standard: All "dots" are removed.
8. Spray fragrance, or open a window, to rid the bathroom of "new plastic odor."
   - ◆ Standard: "New plastic odor" is gone.

<u>Supporting Knowledge:</u>

- ◆ Describe the steps in hanging a shower curtain.
- ◆ Explain when to ensure that the shower curtain design is facing the appropriate direction.
- ◆ List two ways to rid a bathroom of "new plastic odor."

<u>Supporting Attitude(s):</u>

- ◆ Advocate using a process to hang a shower curtain so that it is done correctly the first time.
- ◆ Commit to buying and hanging a new shower curtain whenever circumstances (guests, mildew) warrant the need.

<u>Resources:</u>

- ◆ New plastic shower curtain
- ◆ Plastic curtain hangers
- ◆ Shower rod
- ◆ Bathtub
- ◆ Stool (for shorter people to stand on when placing hangers on shower rod)
- ◆ Fragrance spray

<u>**Job Environment Description:**</u>

The bathroom can be a cramped area for this operation. In some bathrooms, the new-plastic odor of the shower curtain can be overpowering, so a fan or other form of ventilation might be needed. Short people will need a stool to reach the shower rod comfortably. For some people, reaching up to the rod repeatedly to attach the hanger is uncomfortable, and they might need short breaks. This can be a hurried operation in some instances (for example, guests are coming, or a shower is needed immediately).

<u>**JOB PERFORMANCE OBJECTIVE:**</u>

Given a new plastic shower curtain, plastic curtain hangers, shower rod, bathtub, stool, and fragrance spray, hang a new shower curtain, so that the folds/wrinkles are beginning to disappear, little plastic filler dots have been removed from the shower curtain holes, the shower curtain design is facing out into the bathroom, the curtain is spread out over the length of the rod, all dots are removed from the bathtub, and the new-plastic odor is gone.

As you examine figures 4-2 and 4-3, you might think, "This isn't how I would describe the task of developing legal job interview questions," or "This isn't how I would hang a shower curtain." That's because you yourself are a content expert on these two skills (from your own background and experience), but you were not the content expert used as the source for these two task analyses! Often there are multiple ways of implementing a task correctly—particularly if it is a soft skill.

The "correct" content of a job task analysis is determined by the subject matter expert (SME) who provides the information (and the thoroughness of the individual needs assessor who conducts the task analysis). An SME can be an acknowledged expert in the field (internal or external to your organization), an employee who is a star performer in that skill, a reference source such as a book or other document, or even you—if you are an expert in the subject matter. What is important is that the SME is credible and that the SME's version of the task analysis is accurate in the eyes of your client and the organization. You must verify with your client that the job task analysis accurately represents the steps, standards, and environment for the job task before proceeding.

Qualitative Data Collection Methods

Interviews. You can use interviews—one-on-one discussions—to elicit the reactions of the interviewee to carefully focused topics. This data collection method yields subjective and perceptive individual data and illustrative anecdotes. It is most often used to collect data for stages 2 and 4 measures (current performance analysis and learner analysis) and is also used to gather business needs information from your client. Table 4-5 lists some advantages and disadvantages of interviews as a means for collecting data for needs assessment.

Table 4-5. Advantages and disadvantages of interviews for training needs assessments.

Advantages	Disadvantages
• Rich detail • Careful structuring of interview protocol produces consistent data across interviews that can be compared to identify patterns and trends • Can be used to flesh out quantitative data collected in a survey	• Can be time-consuming for the volume of data gained • Interviewees must truly represent the targeted population or the data will be skewed • Frequency of responses does not get at the reason behind the responses (that is, why the respondents felt a certain way) • Interviewer must be careful to record interviewee responses, not interpret

Interview questions must be planned ahead. You must structure the questions to garner the information that is most critical for your needs. Tips for conducting interviews include the following:

▶ Set the interviewee at ease. Begin with general questions and small talk. Slowly move into more specific questions.

▶ Use open-ended questions to get more detailed and rich data. Use closed-ended questions to control the interview and move on.

▶ Ask the interviewee to confirm and specify generalized statements and assumptions that he or she makes.

▶ Take notes. Use a page with interview questions already printed on it (an interview protocol; figure 4-4) and make notes for each question. Show the interviewee your protocol and notes if asked.

▶ Allow pauses for the interviewee to think. Take a brief pause to complete your notes if necessary before moving on.

▶ You may wish to audiotape an interview so that you can check back for the interviewee's exact wording when you are analyzing the data. When you choose to audiotape, assure the interviewee that you are doing it to identify rich anecdotal phraseology and examples that might be significant for the study and for developing learning activities in the later training design. Tell the interviewee that his or her story will not be individually identified and that that tape will be destroyed after the study is complete.

Figure 4-4. Example of a protocol for an interview.

INTERVIEW PROTOCOL
For Potential Participants in Train-the-Trainer Course

Introductory Comments:

Thank you for allowing me some time with you to conduct this interview. Our time together should take _____ minutes *(longer time if in person; shorter time if on telephone)*. The data that I collect in this interview will be anonymous. That means that you will not be identified in any way with your comments. The comments themselves will be used in aggregate form to identify trends in train-the-trainer needs. Specific comments may be quoted in reporting the data if they are particularly illustrative. The respondent will not be identified, and identifying information will be deleted from the quotation. Here's how we will proceed:

- I will mention a train-the-trainer topic to you.
- Please rate the topic first as to how important that topic is to your job. *(1 = not important at all, 5 = critical.)*
- Then, please rate your own self-assessment regarding your current level of knowledge about the topic. *(1 = I don't know very much about this subject, 5 = I am expert in this subject.)*
- Last, for each topic, if you would like to add any comments, please feel free to do so.

Topics:

1. The experiential learning process and discovery learning
   - ○ Importance ranking: _____
   - ○ Self-assessment ranking: _____
   - ○ Comments:

2. Designing lectures
   - ○ Importance ranking: _____
   - ○ Self-assessment ranking: _____
   - ○ Comments:

3. Facilitating lectures
   - ○ Importance ranking: _____
   - ○ Self-assessment ranking: _____
   - ○ Comments:

4. Designing structured exercises
   - ○ Importance ranking: _____
   - ○ Self-assessment ranking: _____
   - ○ Comments:

5. Facilitating structured exercises
   - ○ Importance ranking: _____
   - ○ Self-assessment ranking: _____
   - ○ Comments:

6. Designing case studies
   - ○ Importance ranking: _____
   - ○ Self-assessment ranking: _____
   - ○ Comments:

7. Facilitating case studies
   - ○ Importance ranking: _____
   - ○ Self-assessment ranking: _____
   - ○ Comments:

8. Designing role plays
   - ○ Importance ranking: _____
   - ○ Self-assessment ranking: _____
   - ○ Comments:

(continued on page 54)

Figure 4-4. Example of a protocol for an interview (continued).

9. Facilitating role plays
   - ○ Importance ranking: _____
   - ○ Self-assessment ranking: _____
   - ○ Comments:

10. Designing demonstration/practices
    - ○ Importance ranking: _____
    - ○ Self-assessment ranking: _____
    - ○ Comments:

11. Facilitating demonstration/practices
    - ○ Importance ranking: _____
    - ○ Self-assessment ranking: _____
    - ○ Comments:

12. Other types of learning activities:
    _____
    - ○ Importance ranking: _____
    - ○ Self-assessment ranking: _____
    - ○ Comments:

13. Setting up learning activities: grouping and instructions
    - ○ Importance ranking: _____
    - ○ Self-assessment ranking: _____
    - ○ Comments:

14. Designing activity debriefs
    - ○ Importance ranking: _____
    - ○ Self-assessment ranking: _____
    - ○ Comments:

15. Facilitating activity debriefs
    - ○ Importance ranking: _____
    - ○ Self-assessment ranking: _____
    - ○ Comments:

16. Adjusting facilitation on the fly to compensate for time, experience levels, hot issues, glitches
    - ○ Importance ranking: _____
    - ○ Self-assessment ranking: _____
    - ○ Comments:

17. Personalizing facilitation with stories, analogies, puzzles, and so forth
    - ○ Importance ranking: _____
    - ○ Self-assessment ranking: _____
    - ○ Comments:

18. Choosing media (for example, flipcharts, overheads, handouts, computer, video)
    - ○ Importance ranking: _____
    - ○ Self-assessment ranking: _____
    - ○ Comments:

19. Designing media
    - ○ Importance ranking: _____
    - ○ Self-assessment ranking: _____
    - ○ Comments:

20. Facilitating with media
    - ○ Importance ranking: _____
    - ○ Self-assessment ranking: _____
    - ○ Comments:

21. Developing facilitator guides
    - ○ Importance ranking: _____
    - ○ Self-assessment ranking: _____
    - ○ Comments:

Closing Comments:

- Thank you again for your time. The information you have provided will contribute greatly to an effective train-the-trainer course.
- If you have any additional comments to share, please do so now.

- You will see the results of this needs assessment. (Provide an approximate date and explain how the information will be delivered, whether by the organization's newsletter, email, or some other means of communication.)

Basic Rule 10
To be effective, data collection interviews must be carefully structured.

Data collection interviews can be conducted over the telephone as well. Sometimes this is the only way to get an interview with someone who is hard to reach. Over the phone, you can conduct interviews with people who are far away, and you can use scripts, job aids, and so forth without the interviewee knowing.

There are some disadvantages of telephone interviews. For example, you can't read the interviewee's body language, nor can you tell if the interviewee is distracted or doing something else (reading, typing) while you're trying to conduct an interview. Oftentimes, you have less time to conduct the interview on the phone.

Think About This

When conducting interviews, you must differentiate confidentiality from anonymity. It is anonymity, not confidentiality, that you are promising to the interviewees. Assure interviewees that no one will know what each individual said and that the data collected will be used in aggregate and anecdotal form only.

Critical Incident Interviews. During this specialized type of interview, the needs assessor asks the interviewee to tell stories about times when he or she felt effective or ineffective while performing the targeted skill. The stories are then analyzed for themes that provide indicators of behaviors that contribute to effective performance of the skill. This method is most often used for collecting data for stage 2 measures (desired performance analysis and current performance analysis). Some advantages and disadvantages associated with this method of data collection are listed in table 4-6.

Table 4-6. Advantages and disadvantages of critical incident interviews for training needs assessments.

Advantages	Disadvantages
• Provides rich anecdotal data. • Focuses on the critical behavioral differentiators of excellent performance so the ultimate training will be focused as well • Identifies skills and attributes that are not differentiators of critical performance, thereby supporting a tighter, streamlined training design	• Requires a great deal of time • Very expensive • Individuals who conduct the interviews and implement thematic analysis must be unbiased about what it takes to perform the skill effectively • Must use multiple thematic analysts to ensure reliability

For critical incident interviews, choose a sample of job performers, usually six to 10 individuals. You can focus on star performers (exemplars) if what is important is getting a complete picture of what excellent performance looks like. Or, you can choose two groups: star performers and some folks who are identified by the organization as average performers (though you would not tell them that). By using two groups, you are able to identify differentiating behaviors: those behaviors that only the star performers exhibit and are, therefore, the key contributors to excellent performance of the skill.

Conducting a critical incident interview is different from conducting a normal interview. Use an interview protocol (figure 4-5) and begin by asking a general question such as, "What skills and knowledge do you think it takes to conduct job interviews effectively?" Although the rest of the interview must focus on capturing specific behavioral detail, opening with a general question helps the interviewee feel at ease. Then, for the remainder of the questions use a behavioral protocol: "What did you do?" "What happened?" "Why did you choose to do it that way?" Probe for behavioral details.

Noted

The critical incident method was invented by John C. Flanagan in the 1950s. His original article "The Critical Incident Technique" and a detailed discussion of this method are provided in Zemke and Kramlinger's (1982) book, Figuring Things Out: A Trainer's Guide to Needs and Task Analysis.

Figure 4-5. Example of a critical incident interview protocol.

CRITICAL INCIDENT INTERVIEW PROTOCOL
Interviewing Skills Training Course

1. What skills and knowledge do you think it takes to conduct job interviews effectively?

2. Tell me about a time when you think you did an effective job of conducting a job interview.
   - ◆ Prompting questions, as needed:
     - — How did you know you had done an effective job?
     - — What was the outcome?
     - — How did you prepare? What did you do specifically?
     - — What did you do to begin the interview?
     - — What actions did you take as you conducted the interview?
       - • What precipitated each action?
       - • Why did you take the action?
       - • What thoughts occurred to you as you chose each action during the interview?
     - — How did you end the interview? What did you say and do?
     - — What actions did you take after the interview? When? How?

3. Tell me about a time when you think you did an ineffective job of conducting a job interview.
   - ◆ Prompting questions, as needed:
     - — How did you know you had done an ineffective job?
     - — What was the outcome?
     - — How did you prepare? What did you do specifically?
       - • What parts of this are you satisfied with? Not satisfied? Why?
     - — What did you do to begin the interview?
       - • What parts of this are you satisfied with? Not satisfied? Why?
     - — What actions did you take as you conducted the interview?
       - • What precipitated each action?
       - • Why did you take the action?
       - • What thoughts occurred to you as you chose each action during the interview?
       - • What parts of this are you satisfied with? Not satisfied? Why?
     - — How did you end the interview? What did you say and do?
       - • What parts of this are you satisfied with? Not satisfied? Why?
     - — What actions did you take after the interview? When? How?
       - • What parts of this are you satisfied with? Not satisfied? Why?

Although tape-recording is optional in normal interviews, critical incident interviews must be audiotaped and transcribed. Interviewees' exact phraseology is important in specifically describing the actual behaviors that were exhibited in a specific past event. Any time the interviewee shifts into generalizing or hypothesizing, steer the interview back into focusing on specific behaviors that the interviewee actually exhibited in the story he or she is telling. One sign that the interviewee has moved into generalizing or hypothesizing is the use of present tense. (When people tell a story about something that has occurred, they speak in past tense.) Phrases that signal generalizing or hypothesizing include

- ▶ "I usually . . ."
- ▶ "Here at Whitewater Outfitters, we try to . . ."
- ▶ "I believe that . . ."
- ▶ "My approach is . . ."
- ▶ "I'm the kind of person who . . ."

Basic Rule 11

To ensure reliability of data analysis of critical incident interviews, at least two individuals must be involved in conducting interviews, analyzing the transcripts, and identifying themes. Ideally, one analyst should be internal to the client's organization to provide context for behavioral examples; the other should be external to the client's organization to provide objectivity in analyzing responses.

Focus Groups. This data collection method is a group interview that provides rich data regarding the performers' or learners' job environment, current level of skill and performance, and their perceptions of desired skill and performance level. Focus groups can be used to collect information about stages 2, 3, and 4 measures (current performance, learning needs, learner needs). Table 4-7 lists some advantages and disadvantages of focus groups.

It's important to conduct a focus group on neutral turf, for example, in a conference room that is not in the group's work area. When scheduling people to participate, be general: "We are going to talk about the challenges of conducting job interviews." Specifying the topic too closely ahead of time allows participants to prepare canned responses.

Table 4-7. Advantages and disadvantages of focus groups for training needs assessments.

Advantages	Disadvantages
• Develops hypotheses that can be tested with a larger population through surveys or observation • The facilitator can make note of nonverbal behaviors that accompany statements • Skilled facilitation results in all focus group members being heard rather than just the more verbal participants	• Very time- and resource-intensive • Sometimes a focus group can fall under the influence of particularly verbal members and give the impression of unanimity when it is not necessarily the case • Difficult to facilitate with just one facilitator who must run the group and take notes

Keep the size of a focus group to between five and 12 participants. Consider implementing multiple groups to get segmented data: a group of high performers, a group of average performers, and a group of performers' managers. When facilitating a focus group, use a focus group protocol (figure 4-6), and move from general to specific questions. For example, start with, "How are job interviews conducted here at Whitewater Outfitters?" Gradually move to more specific questions: "In terms of legal or illegal interview questions, what are the trickiest areas, in your opinion?"

Use questions that encourage the participants to speak up while you stay quiet as much as possible. Don't convey via verbal or nonverbal communication your agreement or disagreement with any statements offered by the participants, and don't interject your own comments about the subject. Document the data: Have someone take notes on flipcharts or on paper (preferably not you because you have enough to do facilitating the group), or consider tape recording. If you decide to tape the sessions, begin by offering assurances regarding anonymity and stating that the tape will be destroyed after it is transcribed.

Observation. This data collection method involves sitting with and observing star performers, experts, or average performers. More advanced versions of this method include

Basic Rule 12

Ensure that the data from focus groups will be worth the effort because this is a time-consuming and costly data collection method.

Figure 4-6. Example of a focus group protocol.

FOCUS GROUP PROTOCOL
Interviewing Skills Needs Assessment

Introduction:

◆ Purpose of the needs assessment

◆ How the data will be used

◆ How and why you were chosen

◆ Ask permission to tape record the session

◆ Ask participants to introduce themselves, tell what part of the organization they work in, and how long they have been with the organization

Questions:

◆ How are job interviews conducted here at Whitewater Outfitters?

◆ What do you think is effective in how interviews are conducted here? What do you think is ineffective?

◆ What is your assessment of the outcomes of the interviewing process here (that is, the quality of the new hires)?

◆ How did you learn to conduct job interviews?

◆ How do you prepare for conducting job interviews?

◆ What steps do you take in conducting an interview?

◆ In terms of asking legal and illegal interview questions, what are the trickiest areas?

◆ Once the interviewing process is over, how do you make hiring decisions?

◆ What parts of interviewing would you like to be able to do better? In what ways?

---

time-and-motion studies and human factors studies—the tools of industrial engineers. In this method, an observer watches the job performer and documents each step that the performer implements in the performance of a task, including movements, amount of time for each step, and standards for successful performance. You can use observation to collect data on stage 2 measures (current and desired performance). Table 4-8 offers some advantages and disadvantages of this data collection method.

Basic Rule 13

Observation reveals *what* and *how* performance should be implemented; accompanying observation with interviews identifies the *why* behind performance, as well.

Table 4-8. Advantages and disadvantages of observation for training needs assessments.

Advantages	Disadvantages
• Excellent for assessing training needs for physical/psychomotor skills • Creates a step-by-step procedure (algorithm) that can be standardized for all learners in the form of a flowchart, diagram, graphic, list of steps, or a job aid • If the observer notes job environment conditions that help or hinder performance, these can be included in the data	• Sometimes difficult to identify where a specific task begins and ends • Misses the performer's mental processes in making choices at each step unless accompanied with an interview • Some performers may act differently than they would normally simply because they know they are being watched (known as the Hawthorne Effect); interviewing the performer after observation and asking why certain things were done in certain ways can help control for tnis effect

Observation accompanied by interviews can produce tools known as algorithms. An algorithm depicts both physical steps/behaviors and the thought processes that support those steps. Figure 4-7 is an example of an algorithm depicting the skill of hanging a shower curtain. Notice that it includes both the steps and standards from the original task analysis as well as patterns for internal decision making about the task steps.

Statistics Versus "Sadistics"

You've probably noted in this chapter the use of terms like "sample," and "population," and you have been exhorted more than once to ensure that the audience sample you research is truly representative of the audience population. Does this mean that you might have to enter that other "sadistics" realm of sampling techniques?

Perhaps.

If you are conducting a needs analysis for a small (one- or two-class) "population" and want to implement a survey, you'll be able to cover the entire population. For interviews, focus groups, or observation, you can ensure representativeness by drawing your subjects from differing workgroups or backgrounds. Keep in mind that your training population is not a random representation of the organization's population anyway because they all possess the selected common characteristic of needing the skills that will be taught in the training course.

Figure 4-7. Example of an algorithm resulting from observation.

Algorithm for Hanging a Shower Curtain

Take the new curtain out of the plastic cover

Wrinkled?

YES   NO

Shake curtain until
wrinkles fall out.

Open the package of plastic hangers.

Are little plastic "filler dots" removed from all holes in the curtain?

YES   NO

Remove all "filler dots"
from curtain holes.

Are you tall enough to reach the curtain pole?

YES   NO

Get a stool and stand
on it.

Hold curtain so that the designed side is facing outward, toward you.

Place the hook part of the first hanger in the first hole of the curtain.

Hang the curved part of the first hanger on the shower rod.

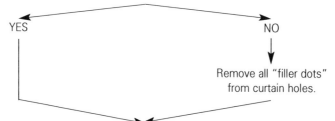
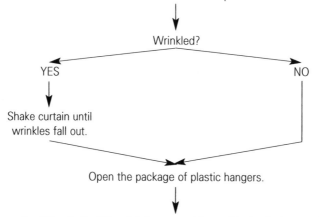

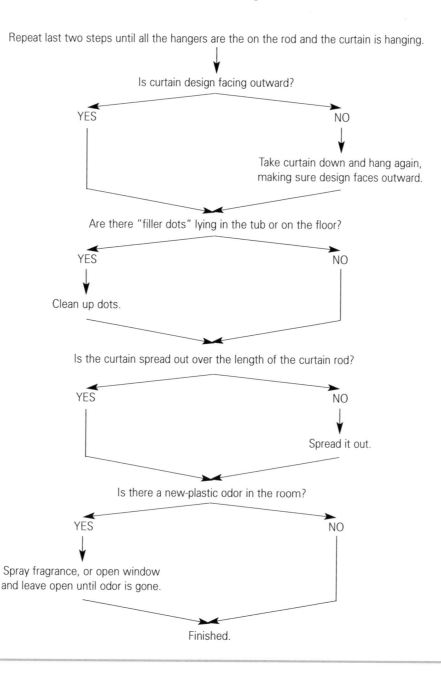

Repeat last two steps until all the hangers are the on the rod and the curtain is hanging.

Is curtain design facing outward?

YES — NO

Take curtain down and hang again, making sure design faces outward.

Are there "filler dots" lying in the tub or on the floor?

YES — NO

Clean up dots.

Is the curtain spread out over the length of the curtain rod?

YES — NO

Spread it out.

Is there a new-plastic odor in the room?

YES — NO

Spray fragrance, or open window and leave open until odor is gone.

Finished.

If your training population is large (say, all first-line supervisors in a very large corporation, which could be any number from 100 to 10,000), you will want to implement sound statistical sampling techniques so that you obtain representative data. There are references in the Additional Resources section that can assist you in this endeavor. Another suggestion, should you have need of moderately advanced (or in some cases, even basic) statistical analysis, is to hire a statistician or statistics graduate student to implement the statistics-related tasks in your needs assessment study.

Basic Rule 14

Be a good planner and consumer of statistical analysis—not a statistician.

Completing the Data Collection Plan

To continue developing the data collection plan, the needs assessor identifies a potential data collection method for each data source and lists these potential methods in the "Potential Data Collection Methods" column of the plan.

When the data collection plan is complete to this point, it may appear in some cases that the data source and the data collection method are one and the same. This happens most often when referring to extant data. For example, if you are going to analyze data on absenteeism from the HR department, the item in the data source column will say something like "extant data on absenteeism from HR." The corresponding item in the potential data collection method column should say "analysis of extant data on absenteeism from HR." The two items are almost the same but not quite. The first item names the resource (person, department, report) that will provide the data; the second item describes what you will do to collect it, if you ultimately choose that method. If you find two corresponding items in the two columns that look exactly the same, one (or both) should be delineated more clearly.

When you've reached this point in your data collection plan, you will likely have many more methods in the "Potential Data Collection Method" column of the plan than you can possibly implement. That is good; it means you have remained open throughout the thought process and have multiple methods from which to choose.

Another observation you may make as you wrap up the data collection plan is that data sources are repeated; that is, some data sources are listed more than once in answer to different data collection questions. Although this repetition may appear unnecessary, it is actually quite important: It guides you in identifying all the data you need from each source so you can prepare to collect all the data at one time from each source.

Table 4-9 summarizes all data collection methods described in this chapter and outlines their most common uses in needs assessment data collection.

Table 4-9. Summary of data collection methods and purposes.

Method	Purpose	Quantitative or Qualitative
Extant Data	• Business needs • Performance needs	Quantitative
Surveys	• Current performance • Current knowledge and skill mastery • Learning needs • Learner needs	Quantitative
Assessments and Tests	• Current performance • Current knowledge and skill mastery • Perceptions of current knowledge and skill	Quantitative
Job Task Analysis	• Required performance • Required learning	Qualitative and Quantitative
Interviews	• Current performance • Learner needs	Qualitative
Critical Incident Interviews	• Required performance • Current performance	Qualitative
Focus Groups	• Current performance • Learning needs • Learner needs	Qualitative
Observation	• Required performance • Current performance	Qualitative

Getting It Done

Knowing the characteristics and advantages and disadvantages of all of the data collection methods available to you will help you identify the best potential methods for your needs assessment.

So, how are things going with Chris back at Whitewater Outfitters? The case study continues in exercise 4-1.

Exercise 4-1. The Whitewater Outfitter case study (part 3).

First, flip back to the data collection plan that you started in exercise 3-1. Compare your data collection questions and data sources to the ones that Chris was able to identify in the following data collection plan (table 4-10). If you identified most of the same responses as Chris, congratulations! If you missed a few, go back to exercise 3-1 and work your way through the information in Chris's interview with Stewart, and see how Chris translated that information to the partial data collection plan shown here.

Now Chris must identify potential data collection methods and while doing so must remember the caveat about not narrowing down the choices too soon. It is not yet the time to choose the methods that will be implemented. Use the information presented in this chapter to help Chris identify some potential data collection methods and list them in the column of the data collection plan (table 4-10) under "Potential Data Collection Method(s)." When you have finished, check your ideas against the next step of Chris's data collection plan in table 4-11.

Chris knows that, practically speaking, not all these data collection initiatives can be implemented because of a shortage of time and resources (and Chris is only one person). Now Chris must decide which methods will provide the most useful data, and which methods will provide the most data at multiple needs assessment stages. In other words, which methods are optimal in terms of providing the best and the most data with the least amount of resources committed?

What methods should Chris choose from the "Potential Data Collection Method(s)" column to be listed in the final column to signify the final choices of data collection methods in the completed data collection plan? List your responses in the rightmost column of the data collection plan in table 4-11.

Table 4-10.

DATA COLLECTION PLAN

PROJECT: Interviewing Skills for Team Leaders, Davidson City Plant, Whitewater Outfitters

Needs Assessment Stage	Questions to Be Answered	Data Source	Potential Data Collection Method(s)	Data Collection Method
Stage 1: Business Needs	a. What are the expected revenues for the City Slicker line?	a. L.K. Stewart, client		
	b. How much of the expected revenues is the Interview Skills Training for team leaders expected to impact?	b. L.K. Stewart, client		
	c. How much of the current turnover can be attributed to the team leaders' current interviewing skills?	c. Tracy Waddell, HR, and HR extant data (turnover data, exit interviews, industry data)		
	d. How much of the retail store and customer complaints can be attributed to poor quality product caused by employees who are not good matches for their jobs because of poor hiring decisions and interviewing skills on the part of the team leaders?	d. Riley Johnson, Complaint Center; Syd Diaz and Morgan Ciscyk, other team leaders		
	e. How many of the four EEO complaints in the current fiscal year are due to illegal interview questions?	e. Tracy Waddell, HR, and HR extant data		

(continued on page 68)

Table 4-10 (continued).

DATA COLLECTION PLAN

PROJECT: Interviewing Skills for Team Leaders, Davidson City Plant, Whitewater Outfitters

Needs Assessment Stage	Questions to Be Answered	Data Source	Potential Data Collection Method(s)	Data Collection Method
Stage 2: Performance Needs	a. What is the required performance for effective interviewing?	a. Tracy Waddell, HR		
	b. What does that performance "look like"?	b. Other "expert" HR staff, external HR resources (books, off-the-shelf training, other experts)		
	c. How do the team leaders currently conduct interviews?	c. Syd Diaz and Morgan Ciscyk, other team leaders, current team members who have been hired in the last year		
	d. What is the team leaders' job environment like?	d. Syd Diaz and Morgan Ciscyk, other team leaders		
Stage 3: Learning Needs	a. What is the skill gap between team leaders' current performance and ideal performance?	a. Expert HR staff, external HR resources (books, off-the-shelf training, other experts)		
	b. What skills and knowledge must the team leaders learn?	b. Expert HR staff, external HR resources (books, off-the-shelf training, other experts)		

DATA COLLECTION PLAN

PROJECT: Interviewing Skills for Team Leaders, Davidson City Plant, Whitewater Outfitters

Needs Assessment Stage	Questions to Be Answered	Data Source	Potential Data Collection Method(s)	Data Collection Method
Stage 4: Learner Needs	a. What are the team leaders' backgrounds in interviewing skills?	a. Syd Diaz and Morgan Ciscyk, other team leaders		
	b. How do these learners learn best? What learning activities work best for them?	b. Syd Diaz and Morgan Ciscyk, other team leaders, former instructors, extant data from former training evaluations		
	c. How do the team leaders feel about the value of interviewing skills to this corporate strategy and hiring push?	c. Syd Diaz and Morgan Ciscyk, other team leaders		
	d. How do these learners feel about the prospect of attending interview skills training?	d. Syd Diaz and Morgan Ciscyk, other team leaders		

Table 4-11.

DATA COLLECTION PLAN

PROJECT: Interviewing Skills for Team Leaders, Davidson City Plant, Whitewater Outfitters

Needs Assessment Stage	Questions to Be Answered	Data Source	Potential Data Collection Method(s)	Data Collection Method
Stage 1: Business Needs	a. What are the expected revenues for the City Slicker line?	a. L.K. Stewart, client	a. Interview Stewart	
	b. How much of the expected revenues is the Interview Skills Training for team leaders expected to impact?	b. L.K. Stewart, client	b. Interview Stewart	
	c. How much of the current turnover can be attributed to the team leaders' current interviewing skills?	c. Tracy Waddell, HR, and HR extant data (turnover data, exit interviews, industry data)	c. Interview Waddell; analysis of extant data	
	d. How much of the retail store and customer complaints can be attributed to poor quality product caused by employees who are not good matches for their jobs because of poor hiring decisions and interviewing skills on the part of the team leaders?	d. Riley Johnson, Complaint Center; Syd Diaz and Morgan Ciscyk, other team leaders	d. Interview Johnson; analysis of extant data; interview Diaz and Cisyk; interview team leaders; survey of team leaders; focus group of team leaders	
	e. How many of the four EEO complaints in the current fiscal year are due to illegal interview questions?	e. Tracy Waddell, HR, and HR extant data	e. Interview Waddell; analysis of extant data; survey of recent employee hires; survey of former employees	

DATA COLLECTION PLAN

PROJECT: Interviewing Skills for Team Leaders, Davidson City Plant, Whitewater Outfitters

Needs Assessment Stage	Questions to Be Answered	Data Source	Potential Data Collection Method(s)	Data Collection Method
Stage 2: Performance Needs	a. What is the required performance for effective interviewing?	a. Tracy Waddell, HR	a. Interview Waddell	
	b. What does that performance "look like"?	b. Other "expert" HR staff, external HR resources (books, off-the-shelf training, other experts)	b. Interview experts and resources; research resources	
	c. How do the team leaders currently conduct interviews?	c. Syd Diaz and Morgan Ciscyk, other team leaders, current team members who have been hired in the last year	c. Interview Diaz and Ciscyk; observe Diaz and Ciscyk; interview team leaders; focus group of team leaders; observe team leaders; survey recent new hires; interview recent new hires; analysis of exit interview data (HR extant data)	
	d. What is the team leaders' job environment like?	d. Syd Diaz and Morgan Ciscyk, other team leaders	d. Interview Diaz and Ciscyk; observe Diaz and Ciscyk; interview team leaders; focus group of team leaders; observe team leaders	

(continued on page 72)

Table 4-11 (continued).

DATA COLLECTION PLAN

PROJECT: Interviewing Skills for Team Leaders, Davidson City Plant, Whitewater Outfitters

Needs Assessment Stage	Questions to Be Answered	Data Source	Potential Data Collection Method(s)	Data Collection Method
Stage 3: Learning Needs	a. What is the skill gap between team leaders' current performance and ideal performance? b. What skills and knowledge must the team leaders learn?	a. Expert HR staff, external HR resources (books, off-the-shelf training, other experts) b. Expert HR staff, external HR resources (books, off-the-shelf training, other experts)	a. Interviews, research b. Interviews, research	
Stage 4: Learner Needs	a. What are the team leaders' backgrounds in interviewing skills? b. How do these learners learn best? What learning activities work best for them?	a. Syd Diaz and Morgan Ciscyk, other team leaders b. Syd Diaz and Morgan Ciscyk, other team leaders, former instructors, extant data from former training evaluations	a. Interview Diaz and Ciscyk; observe Diaz and Ciscyk; interview team leaders; focus group of team leaders; observe team leaders b. Interview Diaz and Ciscyk; interview team leaders; focus group of team leaders; observe team leaders; analysis of past training evaluation data	

DATA COLLECTION PLAN

PROJECT: Interviewing Skills for Team Leaders, Davidson City Plant, Whitewater Outfitters

Needs Assessment Stage	Questions to Be Answered	Data Source	Potential Data Collection Method(s)	Data Collection Method
Stage 4: Learner Needs (continued)	c. How do the team leaders feel about the value of interviewing skills to this corporate strategy and hiring push? d. How do these learners feel about the prospect of attending interview skills training?	c. Syd Diaz and Morgan Ciscyk, other team leaders d. Syd Diaz and Morgan Ciscyk, other team leaders	c. Interview Diaz and Ciscyk; interview team leaders; focus group of team leaders; observe team leaders d. Interview Diaz and Ciscyk; interview team leaders; focus group of team leaders; observe team leaders	

It's time to shift from Whitewater Outfitters back to your own organization now. Please go back to the photocopy you made of figure 3-2, where you have already listed your data collection questions and your data sources for a training needs assessment project that you are working on right now, or one that you know you will be working on in the future. It's time to list some potential data collection methods in the next column. Fill in that column and stop there. You'll have a chance to select your final data collection methods and complete the plan in the next chapter.

Now that you have completed three of your four critical data collection decisions, it is time to choose the methods that you will actually implement.

5

Data Collection Implementation

What's Inside This Chapter

In this chapter, you'll learn:

▶ Factors that assist you in choosing the most effective data collection methods for your needs
▶ Tips for implementing data collection
▶ Why collecting data from multiple sources and at multiple stages is critical to your ultimate training design.

Choosing Data Collection Methods

Another critical part of step 4 of the data collection process is choosing (from the list in the "Potential Data Collection Methods" column of your data collection plan) the data collection methods that will work best in your situation to gain optimal information. You should choose both quantitative and qualitative methods so that your data sets complement each other. There are several factors that you should consider in making data collection method choices. Some important ones are identified and described in table 5-1.

Basic Rule 15

Choose both quantitative and qualitative data collection methods.

Table 5-1. Some factors to consider when selecting data collection methods.

Factor	Considerations
Time Needed	• What is the timeframe for your data collection process? How quickly must the training be designed and implemented? • How much time do you have available to conduct the data collection, keeping in mind your other commitments? • How much time does each data collection method take to implement?
Other Resources Needed	• How much of other employees' time will be needed to assist in actual data collection for each method? • How much of other employees' time will be needed as subjects of each data collection method (that is, interview subjects, survey respondents, and so forth)? • What commitments in terms of other organizational resources (clerical time, equipment, tools, disruption of the work process, for example) are necessary for each method?
Other Costs	• How much will it cost to buy equipment, software, assessment tools, and so forth to implement a particular data collection method? • Are there any fees for external services for conducting interviews, inputting data, transcribing tapes from interviews or focus groups, carrying out statistical analysis, or other activities? • Are there travel expenses necessitated by implementing the selected data collection method?
Essentialness	• Is a specific data collection method one of only a few (or perhaps the only method) that can obtain a needed data set? • Could other data collection methods yield the same data?
Availability of Data Sources	• For each data collection method, which data sources will have easy access (extant data and/or people are easily obtained)? Which sources will take time and resources to gain access? Is appropriate leverage available to assist in gaining access? • Are there internal political implications that apply to certain methods or certain data sets? • What time of year or part of the organization production cycle is it? Access to people, data, and the work environment can be limited if it is the organization's busy season or if it is a time of year when people are away (vacations, holidays, and so forth). • How willing is your client to help you gain access to data sources for each method? (For example, a client may be more willing to allow an email survey than a series of interviews due to perceived disruption of work.)

Factor	Considerations
Logistics	• Are data sources located at multiple sites? Will you have to travel to gather data?
	• How essential are the data collection methods that require travel? Would another method suffice? (For example, can you conduct telephone interviews with people who are at other sites rather than conduct them face-to-face?)
	• Is there technology (email, videoconferencing) available in the organization to assist with logistical issues? If so, will you need assistance in managing the technology or do you already know how to use it?
	• Is there appropriate space in the organization to conduct each data collection method (for example, a private room for interviews, a place to observe work without being intrusive)?
Needs Assessor's Skill Level	• Are there some methods in which you have more experience and expertise? When you have a choice of methods, it can save time and resources to use a method that you know and can do well.

Here are a couple of thoughts about table 5-1: First, the concept of essentialness regarding data collection methods is about the uniqueness of the data that a particular method offers you. It does not mean the same thing as importance or significance of the data being collected. For example, job task analysis would be considered highly essential because it provides data on performance standards (how well each step of a task should be completed)—and very few data collection methods do that. An interview would be considered a less essential method because some of the same data can be obtained from a survey or focus group.

Second, the table indicates that the needs assessor's skill level is another factor to consider, but it is a double-edged sword. If you have expertise and are comfortable with using particular data collection methods, you can probably apply them quite efficiently. But, there is also a downside to using only data collection methods in which you have expertise. You've probably heard the expression "When you get a new hammer, everything in the world looks like a nail." That's what can happen when you continue to choose only data collection methods that you are most familiar with. It becomes very tempting to use the same methods over and over, even when they might not be the best choices. If you reach an unbiased conclusion that a method in which you have little expertise is the best one for the need, it's time to learn how to implement that method. Take the time to teach yourself, seek training that will help you learn it, or hire an expert and "shadow" that person to learn how to implement that data collection method. The extra effort spent will be worth it.

Third, remember to collect only data that you will actually use. Training needs assessment is not the same as pure research. Your job is to help the client take action to resolve a problem, capitalize on an opportunity, or support a business strategy. Your job is to collect enough data to ensure that the ultimate training intervention will support the client's ability to take appropriate action.

Basic Rule 16

Choose to implement data collection methods that will get you the best data with optimal expenditure of resources. Consider time, other resources, financial costs, essentialness, data source availability, logistics, and your own skill level.

Table 5-2 provides a summary of the criteria above as they apply to the most commonly used data collection methods. As you examine the table, you'll likely notice an interesting paradox: In many cases, a data collection method that provides highly essential data also requires great expenditures of resources in terms of time, money, person-hours, or other resources. Conversely, methods that tend to provide less essential data usually require lower resource expenditures. Does this mean that you should only choose methods that provide highly essential data? No. First, remember that essentialness of a data collection method in this context means how unique the data collected is; it does not signify the importance of the data. Second, even if you wanted to do so, you don't have the resources to implement all of the "essential" methods for one project! So, judiciously select one or two essential (and resource-consuming) methods and augment these with less resource-intensive methods.

Table 5-2 compares the feasibility of data collection methods across the selection criteria discussed in this chapter. Note that the rightmost column labeled "Needs Assessor's Skill Level" is blank. That must be filled in by the individual needs assessor.

Implementing Your Data Collection

At last you are finally ready to collect your data. Here are some tips to help you implement the process efficiently and effectively.

▶ *Double-check.* Make a last quick pass over your choices and your reasons for choosing each method. Don't be afraid to make last-minute adjustments before you get started. It is important to be sure you have chosen methods that will optimize your time, access to resources, and the ultimate value of the data.

Table 5-2. Criteria for choosing data collection methods.

Listed below are data collection methods and high, medium, and low rankings for their feasibility across the selection criteria discussed in this chapter. Note that the rightmost column labeled "Needs Assessor's Skill Level" is blank. That must be filled in by the individual needs assessor.

Data Collection Method	Time Needed	Other Resources Needed	Other Costs	Availability of Data Sources	Logistics	Essentialness of Data	Needs Assessor's Skill Level
Extant Data	Low	Low	Low	High	Medium	Medium	
Surveys	Medium to High[1]	Medium to High[2]	Medium to High[3]	Medium	Medium	High	
Assessments/Tests	Low	Low to High[4]	Low to High[5]	High	Low	High	
Job Task Analysis	High	Medium	Low[6]	Medium	Low	High	
Interviews	Medium to High	Low	Low	High	Low[7]	Medium	
Critical Incident Interviews	High	High	High	Medium	Low	High	
Focus Groups	High	Medium	Low	Medium	Medium	Medium	
Observation	High	Low	Low	Medium	Low	Medium	

[1] Medium to administer; high to analyze.
[2] Depending on whether other resources must be used to design, enter data, conduct statistical analysis.
[3] Depending on whether resources to design, enter data, conduct statistical analysis must be purchased.
[4] Low if test/assessment already exists; high if test/assessment must be constructed.
[5] Low if test/assessment already exists; high if test/assessment must be constructed.
[6] Medium if external job analyst is hired.
[7] Can be high if subjects are geographically dispersed; consider telephone interviews instead.

▶ *Make a plan.* Develop a calendar, timeline, flowchart, or some other tool to help you stay on track and remind you that you have a deadline to complete data collection. Monitor your progress on the plan as you go along.

▶ *Be flexible.* One of the nice things about having a plan is that you'll know when you must deviate from it. Accept the fact that things happen in organizational life that are out of your control, and prepare to adjust your data collection as you go along. Did one segment take longer than you thought it would, causing you to implement another segment more quickly than you planned? Are there alternative data collection methods that can be used if it turns out that the one you selected isn't feasible? Can people without access to email receive a paper survey? Also, try to implement the most essential methods first, in case circumstances force you to cut the data-gathering process short.

▶ *Include your client regularly and frequently.* It goes without saying that your client must approve your data collection plan. Then, you must also report back to the client periodically about your progress. It doesn't have to be a formal report; even a voicemail message or email will do. By keeping in touch with the client, if you must change your plan due to organizational circumstances, the client will know about it and can help you get access to alternative data sources. By sharing tidbits of information gathered along the way, you can pique the client's interest in the process and the eventual results, demonstrate the value in the process, and build your credibility. Finally, if you discover data items that are contradictory, the client can help provide context and meaning.

▶ *Keep your own interpretations and experiences out of the data collection.* This is a critical caveat. Your data must be objective or your ultimate data analysis will not be accurate. There are many points at which it is tempting to augment the data with your own views; for example, you try to "help" an interviewee by interpreting what is said by saying something like "So what you really mean is . . ." rather than saying "Can you tell me more about that?" Resist the temptation to add your two cents' worth.

▶ *Be objective.* Avoid structuring data collection to play on your hunches. For example, you get a hunch during an initial interview with a client that part of a performance problem is obsolete equipment. Asking a question in an interview or survey like "What problems have you had with equipment?" is leading and plays too closely on your hunch. Instead, the question might be "What keeps you from achieving the results that are expected of you?" If part of the problem is obsolete equipment, it will come out. Your opportunity to test hunches is in data analysis, not data collection.

▶ *Use extant data correctly.* It's already been said that extant data is rarely if ever collected for your purposes, so you must infer from that data and take steps to validate the inferences if necessary. For example, if many employees said in exit interviews that one of the reasons they left the organization is that the company's benefits program isn't as good as other companies', this is important information. However, it isn't necessarily true information. It means that many of the employees who left *believe* that it's true. Check it out with another data source, or address it in your recommendations (chapter 7).

▶ *Use others to achieve reliability.* If possible, involve other people in some of the data collection to help control for any bias you might have. Have others conduct some of the interviews or take a look at extant data. You can use co-workers from the training or HR department, or your client may provide access to a manager who has an interest or stake in the project.

▶ *Plan how you will share the data when data collection is complete.* Work with your client to decide how the data will be shared with the sources who cooperated with you in the data collection process. Nothing irks people more than being asked for their opinion and then hearing nothing more about it. You and your client have the prerogative to decide what data and how much of it to share, but some kind of follow-up must happen or credibility can be damaged.

▶ *Skim or sample the data as it is being gathered.* If any unique or significant information appears, there is still time to focus subsequent data collection on validating that information or on gathering more of it.

▶ *Stop when you get repetitive data.* There's no rule that says you must complete all the data collection methods in your plan. It has already been mentioned that you might have to cut data collection short because of circumstances. You can also stop when the data trends become so clear that it is likely that more data will simply provide the same information. If the first 10 interviewees said the same thing (and your sample is representative), the last five interviewees will probably say the same thing as well.

Noted

What if you want to collect data at multiple stages from the same source? Say, for example, you know that from a sample group of learners you can gain information about (1) their current skills; (2) what they would like to do better in terms of their job performance needs and learning needs; and (3) their learning styles. Does that mean you must conduct three focus groups with them, or implement three surveys? No. Develop all of your questions for the focus group or survey and administer all of your questions at the same time. Not only is that more efficient for you, but it is more efficient for your data sources as well.

The Ultimate Goal: Generating the Training Design

In chapter 1, the purposes of training needs assessment were examined. Three purposes were discussed:

▶ Training needs assessment places the training need or request in the context of the organization's needs.

▶ It validates and augments the initial issues presented by the client.

▶ It ensures that the ultimate training design supports employee performance and thereby helps the organization meet its needs.

Chapters 1 and 2 presented more detailed discussion regarding the first two purposes of training needs assessment. It is time now to discuss the third purpose, that of ensuring that the ultimate training design will support employee learning and job performance. Training needs assessment serves as input for the ultimate design, but how exactly? What does each stage of needs assessment specifically add to the training design? The following sections address how each stage of needs assessment feeds into the training design and offers some examples of how one organization (a hospital) designed training around needs assessment.

Stage 1: Business Needs Data

How does business needs data support the ultimate training design? When a client makes a training request, it is important to frame that request in the context of business needs. Chapter 1 discussed how that process is important to the training function and to the organization. It is also important for the ultimate training design.

Think About This

One of the struggles faced by all authors of the books comprising ASTD's *Training Basics* series is identifying where to draw the line between the subject matter of one book and the subject matter of a related book in the series. It is a struggle because in the real world of training, all the processes—needs assessment, design, development, delivery, and evaluation—are part of a system in which all these components are interdependent. At times, it is necessary to address when and how one component of the system depends on another component. The discussion in chapter 1 regarding how needs assessment and evaluation are related was one of those instances. This discussion of how needs assessment fits into training design is another.

Using Stage 1 Data in Training Design. You'll recall that business needs involve resolving a problem, capitalizing on an opportunity, or supporting a strategy. The most common sources of business needs information are the client, other leaders of the business, and extant data. Business needs are included in the ultimate training design in the following ways:

▷ Business needs can be used in the introduction of a training course to anchor the course in the business realities and to give the learners the big picture about why they are in the training course.

▷ If learners must be encouraged to buy into the training course, you can help motivate them by providing specific statistics on how increased performance (based on the training course) will affect the business and by how much.

▷ Business need statistics and scenarios can be built into learning activities (case studies, discussions) to make the course relevant and allow the learners to apply their learning to the actual business.

Example. A local hospital has identified a training need to increase "patient interaction skills" of nurse's aides in all units related to maternity services (includes not only a maternity department, but also OB/GYN care, prenatal services, and women's informational and public service events and efforts). There are two business needs driving the training need. First, patient satisfaction statistics in maternity-related areas are slipping (a business problem to resolve), and second, another local hospital has closed down its maternity services, so a prime opportunity exists to become the community's "baby hospital" (a business opportunity to be capitalized upon).

Business needs data provides input into the ultimate patient interaction skills training course design in several different ways. Following are some examples, but you may be able to think of others:

- an introductory learning activity in which the strategic plan for becoming the community baby hospital can be presented
- sharing of patient satisfaction statistics with a subsequent learning activity regarding generating ways to increase those figures
- scenarios or cases that depict interacting with patients in a way that promotes the hospital's baby-related services
- developing or sharing a "patient interaction chain of events," beginning with the planning for pregnancy and ending with postnatal services, which demonstrates all the opportunities the hospital and the learners have to maximize individual patient satisfaction and promote future use of the hospital for maternity-related needs by that patient and all of her contacts (potential hospital customers).

Stage 2: Performance Needs

How does identification of job performance needs data support the ultimate training design? Collecting and identifying data regarding performance needs focuses on what the learners will ultimately have to do back on the job. This data provides information on task steps that employees must perform, the work environment in which they perform, and quality standards for the results they achieve. This information is critical because an effective training design must replicate as closely as possible the skill as it is performed on the job.

Performance needs information must be collected along two lines: What does desired performance look like? What does current performance look like? For desired performance, the most common sources of performance needs information are the client or the managers of the employees, star performer employees, SMEs, and extant data. For current performance needs, the most common sources are the current job performers, the employees' managers, and extant data.

Using Stage 2 Data in Training Design. By comparing the two sets of data on desired and current performance, you can identify the specific performance gap that must be addressed by the training. Identifying this gap is also critical because when training focuses on bridging the performance gap it takes less time by focusing on what the learners really need, the learners are more likely to value the training, the ultimate job performance improves because the true performance gap was addressed, and morale problems associated with irrelevant training are avoided.

Job performance needs data are included in the ultimate training design in the following ways:

- ▷ basis for learning objectives for training design
- ▷ specifics regarding the performance gap to be addressed
- ▷ on-the-job performance measures that will be translated into tests and assessments in the training design
- ▷ indicators for the depth at which to treat knowledge and skills in the training design (identifies which training content can be treated at the knowledge level only and which content must be taken to the skill level in terms of practice and application)
- ▷ simulation of the job environment for learning activities (for example, tools, working conditions, job environment)
- ▷ indicators for transfer learning strategies.

Think About This

Transfer learning strategies are ways of designing and delivering training that encourage application of the learned skills back to the job environment. Reproducing the job environment as closely as possible in the classroom is a transfer strategy: If learners practice a skill in a classroom environment that is very similar to that in the workplace, they are more likely to have confidence in their ability to perform the skill back on the job and, therefore, are more likely to choose to use the skill. Other examples of transfer learning strategies might include action planning for back on the job, or identifying barriers to using the skills in the workplace, and then strategizing tactics to overcome the barriers.

Example. Continuing with the hospital example: Job performance needs assessment data collection regarding the patient interaction skills training course for nurse's aides revealed two specific job performance gaps in this group of employees. First, their job environment is very fast-paced and stressful; they are often interrupted when caring for or interacting with a patient. Consequently, they become distracted and fail to continue or follow up the patient interaction. Second, the nurse's aides don't feel capable of handling patient complaints when the patient is upset or angry; instead, they usually refer these issues to their supervisors. Because it takes time for the supervisor to contact the patient and review the complaint, the result is often intensified patient dissatisfaction because of the delay and suboptimal use of the supervisor's time.

With this information in hand, the training design of the patient interaction skills training course might focus on the following components:

- presentations on the costs related to patient dissatisfaction and referrals of "escalated" patient complaints to supervisors
- role plays in which interactions between a nurse's aide and a patient are enacted and interrupted, accompanied with strategies and job aids to support nurse's aides' skills in handling the interruptions efficiently, and in remembering to follow up to continue a patient interaction when it is interrupted
- skill-based training on handling conflict situations to include steps in handling conflict, scripts for handling the most common patient complaints, and role plays that provide opportunities to practice the skills
- a learning activity that focuses on why it's hard to handle conflict with a patient and why it's important to choose to do it
- transfer strategies that include a job aid (laminated card) containing the conflict handling steps that nurse's aides can refer to on the job and a follow-up brown bag luncheon in which nurse's aides share their experiences, get advice, and celebrate their accomplishments in handling situations more effectively.

Stage 3 Data: Learning Needs

Data regarding learning needs focuses on what the learners must learn in the classroom in order to perform as required on the job. Much of this information is similar to job performance data in that it includes task steps that employees must perform, the work environment in which they perform, and quality standards for the results they achieve. The difference here is that learning needs reflect how the skills must be learned, rather than how they must be performed on the job, and how the skills must be performed in the learning environment in order to master the skills in the job environment.

Learning needs also focus on the gap—only this time, it is the gap in learning rather than in performance. What must the learners *know* in order to *do*? Some of the same data sources are consulted for learning needs as in performance needs: For learning that is required, SMEs, extant data, and star performers are the most common sources. For current learning level, the current job performers are the main source of data, which can be augmented with extant training evaluation data from other courses.

Using Stage 3 Data in Training Design. Learning needs data supports the ultimate training design because it

- ▸ translates learning objectives into learning activities
- ▸ provides content for knowledge-based learning activities
- ▸ provides test and skill assessment items for measurement of learning in the training course, based on how the knowledge and skill are exhibited on the job
- ▸ helps identify the depth and time that should be allotted to each knowledge and skill activity, based on importance.

Example. Learning needs assessment data collection regarding the patient interaction skills training course for nurse's aides revealed, among other things, that (1) there are specific steps to follow in handling a complaint situation that help in resolving it and in lessening the possibility of escalation; (2) an interpersonal skill set is associated with handling conflict and complaint situations; (3) the nurse's aides feel like they are winging it every time they handle a complaint; (4) the better a nurse's aide is at handling interruptions, the more satisfied the aide's patients are; and (5) the more their co-workers interrupt them, the more stressed the nurse's aides feel.

With this information in hand, the training design of the patient interaction skills training course might incorporate the following activities:

- ▸ knowledge-based activities on handling co-worker interruptions
- ▸ knowledge-based activities and job aids on the steps for handling a conflict interaction
- ▸ knowledge-based activities on when to escalate a complaint situation to a supervisor
- ▸ skill-based activities (role plays) on handling interruptions from co-workers

- skill-based activities (role plays) that provide practice both in handling complaints from patients and in handling interruptions from co-workers (the same role plays as mentioned in performance needs analysis with an additional layer of content added based on stage 3 data)
- knowledge test items that reflect job application (for example, nurse's aides often use a reference manual as a regular part of their daily work; in a test in the classroom, they should be "looking up" items in the manual as well; forcing them to answer from memory does not reflect how it's done on the job)
- a short segment on stress reduction techniques (deep breathing, for example).

Stage 4 Data: Learner Needs

Data regarding learner needs focuses on how to make the learning environment conducive to learning for a specific group of learners. The current job performers are the main source of data, with some contributions from extant data in the form of prior training evaluation information.

Using Stage 4 Data in Training Design. How does identification of learner needs data support the ultimate training design? Learner needs data provides the following input into the training design:

- learning styles
- learning activities that are most conducive to the specific learners and their styles
- learners' comfort level with groupings in learning activities (for example, large or small groups)
- pace and energy level of the training (based on time of day, time in learners' work cycle, and learning styles)
- amount of discovery learning to build in (For learners who already know something about the content, activities that allow them to "discover" it followed by summary activities to deliver content are most effective; for learners who are beginners in the content, the opposite progression is most appropriate.)
- sequence of training activities (how to build their learning).

Example. Learner needs assessment data collection regarding the patient interaction skills training course for nurse's aides revealed, among other things, that (1) these learners are primarily visual learners; (2) these learners are used to being on the run and are not accustomed to sitting in a classroom for a long time; (3) the training courses will be offered during the last two hours of their shifts; (4) these learners are uncomfortable with being in front of a group, speaking out, or in other ways being the center of attention; (5) they know very little about handling conflict and complaints; and (6) they are experienced at handling interruption; they just choose not to do it well because it causes more stress for them.

With this information in hand, the training design of the patient interaction skills training course might include the following activities:

- graphic, visual materials in a variety of media
- high energy levels in the facilitator and in activities (plenty of moving around on the part of the facilitator and learners; getting up to work at flipcharts; changing groups to interact with other people)
- small-group discussions (pairs and trios) to increase comfort with speaking up
- role plays beginning with the instructor enacting a role play with learners providing critiques and ending with small group role plays in trios, thereby building intensity and comfort level with the role play activities; no role plays in front of whole group
- content presentation followed by structured activities for "handling complaints" portion
- "discovery" learning for "handling interruptions" portion
- a non-training recommendation that nurse's aides' co-workers be trained or provided incentives to avoid piling more interruptions on those nurse's aides who handle interruptions well (non-training recommendations are discussed in chapter 7).

Getting It Done

To choose the best data collection methods for your needs, you must

- know which data you need and how essential it is
- analyze the potential methods for feasibility
- assess your own skill at implementing each method
- understand what parts of your ultimate training design will require data to complete.

To assess your own level of skill in regard to applying some of the data collection techniques discussed, go back to table 5-2 and fill in your self-ratings in the column marked "Needs Assessor's Skill Level." Now you can use the complete matrix to assist with making data collection method decisions in your own practice.

Next, take a look at exercise 5-1 to see how Chris is progressing with the needs assessment project at Whitewater Outfitters.

Exercise 5-1. The Whitewater Outfitter case study (part 4).

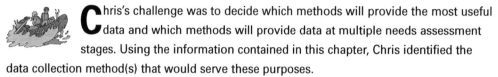 **C**hris's challenge was to decide which methods will provide the most useful data and which methods will provide data at multiple needs assessment stages. Using the information contained in this chapter, Chris identified the data collection method(s) that would serve these purposes.

The methods Chris chose from all the potential methods in the data collection plan are listed in table 5-3. Compare the list you generated at the end of exercise 4-1 to Chris's. If you identified most of the same responses as Chris did, congratulations! If you missed a few, go back to part 3 of the case and work your way through Chris's list of potential data collection methods, and analyze how Chris was influenced to decide upon the final data collection implementation choices listed in the rightmost column of the data collection plan. Note how Chris selected specific data collection methods for the specific needs identified and did not include all data needs in all methods chosen.

Chris then presented the final list to Stewart for approval. Stewart approved the list, and sent emails to the appropriate individuals to prepare the way for Chris's contacts with them. Now, all Chris has to do is implement the data collection process. What tips and warnings would you offer to help Chris implement the data collection efficiently and effectively? List your responses here:

_____

_____

_____

_____

Table 5-3.

DATA COLLECTION PLAN

PROJECT: Interviewing Skills for Team Leaders, Davidson City Plant, Whitewater Outfitters

Needs Assessment Stage	Questions to Be Answered	Data Source	Potential Data Collection Method(s)	Data Collection Method
Stage 1: Business Needs	a. What are the expected revenues for the City Slicker line?	a. L.K. Stewart, client	a. Interview Stewart	• Interview Stewart
	b. How much of the expected revenues is the Interview Skills Training for team leaders expected to impact?	b. L.K. Stewart, client	b. Interview Stewart	• Interview Stewart
	c. How much of the current turnover can be attributed to the team leaders' current interviewing skills?	c. Tracy Waddell, HR, and HR extant data (turnover data, exit interviews, industry data)	c. Interview Waddell; analysis of extant data	• Interview Waddell; analyze turnover data, industry data, exit interview data
	d. How much of the retail store and customer complaints can be attributed to poor quality product caused by employees who are not good matches for their jobs because of poor hiring decisions and interviewing skills on the part of the team leaders?	d. Riley Johnson, Complaint Center; Syd Diaz and Morgan Ciscyk, other team leaders	d. Interview Johnson; analysis of extant data; interview Diaz and Cisyk; interview team leaders; survey of team leaders; focus group of team leaders	• Interview Johnson • Interview Johnson • Small group interview of team leaders, including Diaz and Cisyk • Focus group of team leaders
	e. How many of the four EEO complaints in the current fiscal year are due to illegal interview questions?	e. Tracy Waddell, HR, and HR extant data	e. Interview Waddell; analysis of extant data; survey of recent employee hires; survey of former employees	• Interview Waddell • Analyze EEO report

(continued on page 92)

Table 5-3 (continued).

DATA COLLECTION PLAN

PROJECT: Interviewing Skills for Team Leaders, Davidson City Plant, Whitewater Outfitters

Needs Assessment Stage	Questions to Be Answered	Data Source	Potential Data Collection Method(s)	Data Collection Method
Stage 2: Performance Needs	a. What is the required performance for effective interviewing?	a. Tracy Waddell, HR	a. Interview Waddell	• Interview Waddell
	b. What does that performance "look like"?	b. Other "expert" HR staff, external HR resources (books, off-the-shelf training, other experts)	b. Interview experts and resources; research resources	• Purchase external module
	c. How do the team leaders currently conduct interviews?	c. Syd Diaz and Morgan Ciscyk, other team leaders, current team members who have been hired in the last year	c. Interview Diaz and Ciscyk; observe Diaz and Ciscyk; interview team leaders; focus group of team leaders; observe team leaders; survey recent new hires; interview recent new hires; analysis of exit interview data (HR extant data)	• Interview Diaz and Cisyk • Observe Diaz (one-way mirror) • Focus group of team leaders • Analysis of exit interview data
	d. What is the team leaders' job environment like?	d. Syd Diaz and Morgan Ciscyk, other team leaders	d. Interview Diaz and Ciscyk; observe Diaz and Ciscyk; interview team leaders; focus group of team leaders; observe team leaders	• Observe Diaz (one-way mirror) • Interview Diaz and Cisyk • Focus group with team leaders

DATA COLLECTION PLAN

PROJECT: Interviewing Skills for Team Leaders, Davidson City Plant, Whitewater Outfitters

Needs Assessment Stage	Questions to Be Answered	Data Source	Potential Data Collection Method(s)	Data Collection Method
Stage 3: Learning Needs	a. What is the skill gap between team leaders' current performance and ideal performance?	a. Expert HR staff, external HR resources (books, off-the-shelf training, other experts)	a. Interviews, research	• Interview expert HR staff member • Small group interview with team leaders • Purchased module • Interview with expert HR staff member
	b. What skills and knowledge must the team leaders learn?	b. Expert HR staff, external HR resources (books, off-the-shelf training, other experts)	b. Interviews, research	
Stage 4: Learner Needs	a. What are the team leaders' backgrounds in interviewing skills?	a. Syd Diaz and Morgan Ciscyk, other team leaders	a. Interview Diaz and Ciscyk; observe Diaz and Ciscyk; interview team leaders; focus group of team leaders; observe team leaders	• Focus group with team leaders
	b. How do these learners learn best? What learning activities work best for them?	b. Syd Diaz and Morgan Ciscyk, other team leaders, former instructors, extant data from former training evaluations	b. Interview Diaz and Ciscyk; interview team leaders; focus group of team leaders; observe team leaders; analysis of past training evaluation data	• Focus group with team leaders • Analysis of past training data (extant)

(continued on page 94)

Table 5-3 (continued).

DATA COLLECTION PLAN

PROJECT: Interviewing Skills for Team Leaders, Davidson City Plant, Whitewater Outfitters

Needs Assessment Stage	Questions to Be Answered	Data Source	Potential Data Collection Method(s)	Data Collection Method
Stage 4: Learner Needs (continued)	c. How do the team leaders feel about the value of interviewing skills to this corporate strategy and hiring push? d. How do these learners feel about the prospect of attending interview skills training?	c. Syd Diaz and Morgan Ciscyk, other team leaders d. Syd Diaz and Morgan Ciscyk, other team leaders	c. Interview Diaz and Ciscyk; interview team leaders; focus group of team leaders; observe team leaders d. Interview Diaz and Ciscyk; interview team leaders; focus group of team leaders; observe team leaders	

All right; you have finally implemented your data collection and you have collected your data—now what do you do with it? You'll determine what it all means in chapter 6.

6

Data Analysis Findings

What's Inside This Chapter

In this chapter, you'll learn:

▶ The difference between data analysis findings and data analysis recommendations

▶ The types of findings that are identified for each needs assessment stage

▶ Basic information about the role of statistical analysis in training needs assessment

▶ Discussion of non-training needs assessment findings.

Findings Versus Recommendations

Once you have gathered all your needs assessment data, it is time to extract some meaning from the data. As there are separate thought processes in data collection planning, so there are in data analysis as well. Data analysis (step 5 in the needs assessment process) consists of two thought processes that must be kept distinct:

▶ identifying findings

▶ developing recommendations based on the findings (figure 6-1).

Figure 6-1. The training needs assessment process with step 5 highlighted.

Step 1. Conduct external and organization scan

Step 2. Collect data to identify business needs

Capitalize on an opportunity
Resolve a problem
Support a strategy

Step 3. Identify potential training intervention

Step 4. Collect data to identify performance, learning, and learner needs

Required performance
Learners' current performance
Required skills and knowledge
Learners' current skills and knowledge
Learner needs

Step 5. Analyze data

Identify findings: gaps in performance, skills, and knowledge
Identify recommendations

Step 6. Deliver data analysis feedback

Training recommendations: design and delivery; ROI forecast
Non-training recommendations: work environment, rewards, consequences, work processes

Transition step: Begin training design

What's the difference? To some needs assessors, there isn't much difference, and that's what gets them into trouble. Say, for example, that a needs assessment study focuses on helping a client reduce turnover. One of the findings is that a large majority (80 percent) of employees who have left the organization in the past year cite job stress as their main reason for leaving. Without putting some intellectual distance between this finding and developing a related recommendation, it is very easy to jump to a recommendation that the current employees should undergo stress management training or that their jobs be redesigned to be less stressful. These two potential recommendations are not necessarily supported by the data, but it's easy to make the mistake of thinking that they are.

Findings are pure; they are unaffected by the context of the organization or the needs assessor's biases. Simply put, findings are the *facts* indicated by the data. They present a clear picture of what is going on in the organization. In this example, the finding is that 80 percent of recent ex-employees said a certain thing. The finding doesn't identify why the ex-employees said it; it doesn't indicate whether what they said is true; and it certainly doesn't indicate what should be done about it. The needs assessor will find out these things as the data analysis continues—and when the time comes to identify recommendations.

Basic Rule 17

Don't jump from a finding to a recommendation. Keep these thought processes separate.

Recommendations (discussed in chapter 7) are contextual within the organization and situation, as well as with other data. The findings data provides information about many different organizational aspects in addition to the training need. Recommendations, rather than being pure, are affected by the needs assessor's job role and areas of responsibility. In the example regarding ex-employees' view of benefits, both recommendations are not only flawed, but also are outside the purview of a training professional's role. Does that mean non-training data is not addressed at all in recommendations? No, it means that needs assessment recommendations are carefully crafted based on a number of factors.

Needs assessment data analysis adds value in two ways: by first developing a current picture of what's going on and then by translating the data into action items or recommendations. In fact, this two-part process also provides the framework for how the data analysis findings and recommendations will be shared with the client when you present your report to your client (discussed in chapter 8).

What Does the Data Say?

The first task in data analysis is to classify and summarize your key findings. If your data collection methods were both quantitative and qualitative, you will have both kinds of data to analyze. Quantitative data is usually depicted numerically as frequencies, percentages, or other measures of proportion, as in how many survey respondents said X or Y. Analyzing this data involves determining what the numbers really mean. If 80 percent of survey respondents said X, and 20 percent said Y, what does that mean (not what should be done about it; that's the recommendation part!)?

Qualitative data is usually narrative in form: anecdotes, stories, survey essay questions. Analyzing these kinds of data involves identifying themes, patterns, trends, key ideas, issues, and determining their strength by examining how often those patterns or trends occur. There may even be opportunities to combine qualitative and quantitative data analysis to determine stronger and more robust patterns and themes. For example, how many employees said X or Y on the survey and how many said the same thing during focus groups? Do the proportions match? What key words from the survey were repeated in the focus group? What key words were not repeated?

Data analysis results in findings at all four needs assessment stages. The following sections describe the kinds of findings to expect from your needs assessments.

Stage 1: Business Needs and the Training Intervention

These findings relate to

> - importance of the business goal in the client's overall business plan
> - strength and clarity of the relationship between business issues and the proposed training intervention
> - indicators for how much of the business goals the training intervention should be expected to achieve
> - accuracy of the business indicators in the client's original presenting problem
> - additional business indicators that figure into the situation.

Very rarely, if ever, will a training course alone achieve a change in a business indicator; too many other factors in the environment could also have an effect on the business indicator. For example, say a company introduces a new product and the organization's expectation is that overall company sales will increase by 20 percent in the second quarter after the product is introduced and the new product sales training has taken place. There are many organizational and marketplace factors that can affect the sales of this new product; the new product sales training is but one such factor.

The training professional and client should negotiate what proportion of that 20 percent increase that training alone should be expected to achieve. Allowing the client to assume that training can achieve the entire business goal is a canary-in-the-coal-mine move!

Stage 2: Specific Desired Work Performance

These findings relate to

- results expected from job performers
- how job performers should achieve those results; performance standards
- background information regarding the job environment, tools, and processes used when employees perform the targeted skills
- organizational factors (non-training factors) other than knowledge or skill deficiencies that affect performance
- indicators regarding transfer strategies that might be required in the training design.

Identifying job performance standards for employees who will be in the proposed training is important because this information will be translated into measurement tools during the training course. Some performance standards focus on the *process* of task accomplishment. The assumption is that if a performer accomplishes the task steps in a prescribed way, the task will be done perfectly. Other performance standards focus on the task *product*. In this case, the assumption is that it doesn't matter what steps the performer takes—what matters is that the product produced meets specific quality standards. If it does, then the task will have been done perfectly.

Stage 3: Training Design Information

These findings relate to

- learning objectives
- indicators for learning activities that will replicate the job environment
- background information to replicate the job environment for skill practices

- test items for knowledge assessments
- process and product checklists for skill practice assessments
- how learners value (or not) the skills to be taught
- other attitudinal information about the learners.

Identifying learner attitudes and how they value the skills to be taught is important. As discussed in chapter 5, you're likely to encounter occasions when the training design must include buy-in learning activities—activities to persuade and influence the learners in their attitudes toward the skills and the learning.

Stage 4: Training Delivery Information

These findings relate to

- physical environment indicators
- facilitation process standards.

The physical learning environment plays a big part in helping learners learn. If the environment is not a conducive one, the learners will be distracted and barriers to learning are created. Needs assessment findings will provide information regarding optimal physical aspects of the learning environment. Examples include size, layout, furniture setup and placement, space required for movement or activities, groupings of learners, technological equipment (projectors, television, and so forth), and amenities (refreshments, take-aways) required.

Facilitation process standards are just that—standards for how a training course is to be facilitated. They are standards that guide how the facilitator will teach the training course. Some process standards are generated by the subject matter, the training designer, and the facilitator himself or herself. Examples of these include

- Questions are encouraged.
- Learner questions are first directed back to the learners to give them "first crack."
- Activity debriefings always focus on application back to the job.
- Facilitation is based on principles of adult learning.
- Level of materials for learners is based on their backgrounds and experience.
- Emphasis for different content segments is based on learners' needs.
- Instructional strategy is based on learning preferences of the learners.
- Grouping of learners is based on organizational levels of learners and the implications of information that might be shared during the training.

Other facilitation process standards are generated by information about the learners gleaned in the needs assessment. Examples of learner information and corresponding process standards are provided in table 6-1.

Table 6-1. Examples of facilitation process standards based on learner information.

Learner Information	Process Standards
• Learners are not used to sitting still; their jobs are physically active.	• Learning activities must include physical movement such as changing seats, working on flipcharts, standing up to share information, and so forth.
• Learners are apprehensive about using the skill set in the training; their confidence level is not very high.	• Incorporate several activities that focus on "What barriers make this hard?" and "How can we overcome the barriers?" • Break learning segments into small segments so that learners experience incremental successes.
• Learners have different learning styles.	• Present information in multiple ways to match as many learning styles as possible.

A Short Side Trip to Descriptive Statistical Analysis

It is a rare training professional indeed who entered the field because of his or her excitement about conducting statistical analysis during the needs assessment process! Nevertheless, there are times when statistical analysis of a quantitative set of data (usually found in extant data, test scores, survey responses, and the like) is very useful. Statistical data analysis provides findings and evidence that will drive your recommendations. However, it is you who must attribute meaning to the data; it is meaningless until you do that.

Basic Rule 18

Statistical data is meaningless until meaning is attributed to it.

Descriptive Statistics

The way you attribute meaning to statistical data is through the use of descriptive statistics. Descriptive statistics are methods of interpreting data that enable meaning to be derived. There may be times that you are actually conducting statistical analysis and must determine what the statistics mean. On other occasions you see a reference to statistical analysis in extant data that you have gathered or in a journal article you have read. A basic understanding of descriptive statistics is useful to help you perform your own calculations to guide you in being an intelligent "consumer" of statistical analysis. Following are descriptions of basic descriptive statistical methods:

- ▶ *Interval scale:* A scale in which the difference between two values measured on the scale has the same meaning. This implies that scores may meaningfully be added or subtracted. Example: Test scores on a scale of 0 to 100. Interval scales can also be used in an answer scale on a survey or questionnaire in which the meanings of the various scale levels are defined to be at equal intervals. Example: A survey in which the answers are on a 5-point scale of: 1 = strongly disagree; 2 = disagree; 3 = neither agree nor disagree; 4 = agree; 5 = strongly agree. In this case, the intervals between the scale items are defined to be equal.
- ▶ *Nominal scale:* A type of scale with a limited number of possible outcomes that cannot be placed in any order representing their relative value. Examples: female versus male; age groups.
- ▶ *Reliability:* The extent to which a test or measuring procedure yields the same results on repeated trials.
- ▶ *Validity:* The extent to which a test or measuring procedure measures what it is purported to measure.
- ▶ *Frequency:* The number of times a value appears in a data set.
- ▶ *Mean:* The value that is computed by dividing the sum of a set of terms by the number of terms; also called the average.
- ▶ *Median:* The value in an ordered set of values below and above which there is an equal number of values.
- ▶ *Mode:* The most frequent value of a set of data.
- ▶ *Percentile:* A descriptive scale that demonstrates how a score or measure compares to other measures in the same data set. For example, in a set of test scores, if a specific score is at the 80th percentile, 20 percent of the test

scores in the set are greater than this score and 80 percent of the test scores are less than this score (regardless of the actual numerical value of the test score itself).

▶ *Significance:* A test for determining the probability (*P*) that a given result did not occur just by chance. For example, if the data derived from a set of test scores is "significant at the *P* = .01 level," it means that there is a 1 percent possibility that the test results occurred by chance and a 99 percent possibility that the test results demonstrate a pattern. A *P* value greater than .10 (10 percent possibility that the test results occurred purely by chance) is generally considered to be low significance.

Basic Rule 19

In statistics, "significance" of the data does not mean importance of the data. The term refers to statistical significance—the probability (*P*) that the results occurred purely by chance.

Inferential Statistics

Another set of statistics is called inferential statistics. Rather than describing the data as in descriptive statistics, inferential statistics are used to present various relationships among values in the data set. Conclusions about the data can then be inferred from examination of the statistics.

The most common inferential statistic that you are probably familiar with is standard deviation, which is a measure of how much variability exists in the data set. If the data points are widely scattered or if the data set is small, the standard deviation is going to be greater than if the data points are close together or if the data set is large.

Further exploration of statistical analysis, both descriptive and inferential, is beyond the scope of this book. Several references in the Additional Resources section can provide more detail regarding statistical analysis of needs assessment data.

Using Statistics to Derive Meaning

You've heard the expression, "Statistics don't lie; statisticians do." That's a very cynical way of saying that statistical results can be presented and interpreted in more than one way to achieve different goals. This point will come into play in chapter 8, in which delivering feedback to the client is discussed. However, it fits well into the context of this discussion, too. Consider the following example:

▸ Exit interview data from employees who have left the organization in the past year were analyzed.
▸ The number of ex-employees represented in the data was 40.
▸ Of these 40 ex-employees, 18 (45 percent of total respondents) said that "low salary" was a major reason for their leaving.
▸ Out of those 18, 10 (56 percent of the 18; 25 percent of total respondents) said that "lack of training and development opportunities" was a second major reason for leaving.

Could it be said that "almost half" of the ex-employees cited low salary? Yes, if you want to highlight a salary issue. Could it be said that "less than half" of the ex-employees cited low salary? Yes, if you want to downplay the salary issue. Could it be said that "more than half," or 56 percent, of those who cited low salary also cited lack of training and development opportunities? Yes, if you want to highlight the training and development issue. Could it be said that "only 25 percent" of the total respondents cited the lack of training and development opportunities? Yes, if you want to downplay the training and development issue.

Is each of these findings correct and true? Yes. Is each intended to influence the client in a different direction? Yes. Is it ethical to present data in this manner? You make the call. There is a fine line between influence and manipulation in the world of statistical analysis. Where that line is depends on the situation, the client, and the inherent risk for the training professional in making flawed data interpretations. Here are two suggestions:

▸ When you have statistical analysis that provides indicators that aren't very strong, seek additional corroborating data from your other sources and methods to bolster or refute the statistical analysis.
▸ If it doesn't feel right, it probably isn't.

Your short side trip to descriptive statistical analysis is now complete. It was mentioned earlier that a presentation of the complexity of more than basic statistics is beyond the scope of this book. You are encouraged to educate yourself so that you can understand basic statistical analysis and be a good "statistics consumer." Beyond that, if your needs assessment study truly requires the rigor of more advanced statistical analysis, it is recommended that you hire a statistician—or a statistics graduate student!

Non-Training Needs

Do you remember the scenario presented in chapter 2 about how clients request training and how tempting it is to simply say "Yes, what time?" When that scenario is played out, so-called needs assessment (if any takes place at all) is focused on the training only: What should be the schedule? How many lessons? What learning activities? Because a true needs assessment focuses on job performance and how training can support it, it places the training in the big picture of how it will support the business. And, because data collection and analysis in this case are broader in scope, one inevitable (and highly desired) result is the identification of non-training-related findings as well as training-related findings.

Why is the identification of non-training issues a desired outcome? Whether the focus is on a business problem, opportunity, or strategy, training itself only supports job performance that is related to knowledge and skill deficiencies. Lack of job performance (and the ensuing lack of business results) is usually due to multiple factors, only some of which are related to training.

Clients sometimes make the assumption that training is the only answer. If you allow that assumption to continue, sooner or later results will occur that don't meet

Think About This

Being able to identify non-training issues as barriers to performance is the key to making the leap from training to human performance improvement (HPI). "HPI is . . . a systemic and systematic approach to identifying the barriers that prevent people from achieving top performance . . . . If people are to achieve top-level performance, [you must] optimize all the components of their human performance system. With each barrier in the system, their performance decreases" (Fuller, 1999). The job of the human performance consultant is to remove as many of the barriers as possible or practical through any of a variety of interventions, including training.

the business needs. The client will return to you, saying "My business need wasn't met! Your training didn't work!" Your credibility could be damaged or lost entirely in the eyes of this client.

Instead, in the beginning you negotiate (as much as possible) a proper needs assessment with the client because proper needs assessment focuses on the big picture of job performance and its impact on the business. In so doing, your guiding question is: "If the training itself is an overwhelming success, what else is going on that could prevent improved job performance and thus prevent the attainment of business needs?"

Examples of non-training issues that affect job performance include

- *Tools:* Lack of equipment, not enough for all to use, obsolete equipment
- *Regulations:* Organizational or governmental regulations that prevent people from performing in the way required to achieve business results
- *Organizational structure:* Structure that is too narrowly or broadly defined to allow for required accountabilities and performance
- *Customers:* Changes in customer needs and interests that affect business results
- *External pressures:* Competition, market influences, time of year, weather, political environment, current events
- *Workforce:* Demographics, number of people with desired skill sets, cultural differences, age or generational differences
- *Resources:* Equipment, facilities, people, time, money, work processes, and organizational policies that support desired behaviors
- *Incentives:* Rewards for desired performance are not matched to performers, or worse, there are none; conversely, rewards inadvertently given for lack of performance
- *On-the-job reinforcement:* Lack of practice opportunities, no reward for incremental successes, little or no managerial support
- *Organizational culture:* Non-supportive culture including work and time pressures, contradictory organizational values, insufficient authority
- *Motivation:* Lack of desire to perform (though not lack of skill).

As you can see, there are many potential non-training influences on job performance and, ultimately, organization needs. Because you identify them in data analysis findings, should you make recommendations regarding them as part of the needs assessment process? That question is addressed in chapter 7.

Getting It Done

Data analysis findings are literally what the data means—the facts and indicators that the data signifies to you regarding what is going on in the organization regarding a potential training need. It is important to represent findings in a way that is as unvarnished and unembellished as possible so meaning can be determined.

Exercise 6-1 presents a data set for you to practice calculating the frequency, mean, median, and mode. The answers immediately follow the exercise.

Exercise 6-1. Descriptive statistics practice.

A knowledge test with 100 items was administered to 20 participants. The possible score range for the test was 0 (no correct answers) to 100 (all correct answers). Following are the test scores:

Person A	Person B	Person C	Person D	Person E	Person F	Person G	Person H	Person I	Person J
Score: 98	Score: 100	Score: 87	Score: 63	Score: 60	Score: 79	Score: 87	Score: 52	Score: 84	Score: 91
Person K	Person L	Person M	Person N	Person O	Person P	Person Q	Person R	Person S	Person T
Score: 98	Score: 89	Score: 87	Score: 72	Score: 75	Score: 59	Score: 68	Score: 93	Score: 80	Score: 68

1. What is the frequency distribution for these test scores?

2. What is the mean of these scores?

3. What is the median of these scores?

4. What is the mode of these scores?

Answers

1. The frequency distribution for the test scores is as follows:

Score	Frequency		Score	Frequency
100	1		79	1
98	2		75	1
93	1		72	1
91	1		68	2
89	1		63	1
87	3		60	1
84	1		59	1
80	1		52	1

2. The mean for these scores is the sum of the scores divided by the number of scores:
    1,590 ÷ 20 = 79.5

3. The median for these scores is the value(s) below and above which there is an equal number of values.
    100, 98, 98, 93, 91, 89, 87, 87, 87, **84, 80,** 79, 75, 72, 68, 68, 63, 60, 59, 52 (Double median, which can
    occur)

4. The mode for these scores is the most frequently occurring value: 87. (When there are multiple
    values that occur with the same frequency, the distribution is *bi-modal, tri-modal, or multi-modal.)*

Chris did a good job in identifying the things to watch out for as the data collection implementation began. Now, what does the data show (exercise 6-2)?

Exercise 6-2. Whitewater Outfitters case study (part 5).

 Before beginning the data collection implementation, Chris carefully thought through the process to plan for contingencies:

- Be careful not to "contradict" Stewart in next interview by mentioning hunches.
- Ask Waddell and Johnson what indicators for job interviewing *they* think the extant data they are supplying shows.
- Conduct the joint interview with Diaz and Ciscyk *before* the team leader focus group, to get information to shape focus group questions.
- Ask another training/HR person to assist with conducting the focus group and interpreting focus group results.
- Structure some focus group questions to check out the results of the joint interview with Diaz and Ciscyk.

- Interview Diaz after observation to get at the thoughts that drive interview behaviors.
- Ask someone internal who has a statistical background to help analyze extant data.
- Send a progress report via email to Stewart every few days to report (1) what was done; (2) a few of the most interesting findings; and (3) what will be implemented next.
- Keep track of Stewart's reactions to the progress reports (items that caught interest, ways of expression that were confusing to Stewart, questions Stewart asked in response). These items could be indicators for structuring the needs assessment report to Stewart later.

Compare your list of tips and warnings from exercise 5-1 with Chris's list. If you identified most of the same responses as Chris, congratulations! If you identified even more than Chris, way to go! If you missed a few, go back to the earlier case descriptions in earlier chapters and see if you can spot the indicators for Chris's list above.

Chris then analyzed the data to identify findings. Table 6-2 lists Chris's findings without going into the actual data analysis.

Now your work begins:

1. In the third column, place a checkmark next to the findings that Stewart (the client) was correct about.
2. In the fourth column, indicate with an arrow (→) each finding that represents new information that had not been identified by Stewart.
3. In the fifth column, place a letter T next to each finding that is training related and NT next to each finding that is not training related.
4. In the sixth column, jot down the data source that provided each finding.
5. Now, answer this question:

Given these findings, what should Chris recommend to the client (Stewart)? List your recommendations here.

_____

_____

_____

_____

_____

_____

Table 6-2.

Needs Assessment Stage	Findings	Was Stewart Right (✓)	Was Information New to Stewart (→)?	Training (T) or Non-Training (NT)?	Data Source
Stage 1: Business Needs	• The upcoming hiring push will require strong interviewing skills on the part of the team leaders.				
	• Two of the four EEO complaints in the past fiscal year relate directly to team leaders having asked illegal interview questions.				
	• A glitch in the shipping process has caused 85% of customer and retail store complaints in the past six months. Shipping is not part of the production process.				
	• Turnover is higher than the industry average. There is a direct connection between the higher turnover and the following four factors: — Team leaders are making poor hiring decisions, resulting in turnover due to stress and burnout (in underqualified new hires) and boredom (in overqualified new hires). — A common source of stress for all team members occurs during midday hours when fellow team members take lunch breaks and the same amount of work must be done with fewer people on the line. — Team members are stressed by the large amount of negative and critical feedback they receive from their team leaders regarding the perceived production problems (and team leaders are getting the same negative and critical feedback themselves). — There is a common perception among employees that Eddie Bean's benefits are better than Whitewater Outfitter's benefits.				

Needs Assessment Stage	Findings	Was Stewart Right (✓)	Was Information New to Stewart (→)?	Training (T) or Non-Training (NT)?	Data Source
Stage 2: Performance Needs	• Team leaders must conduct consistent interviews from team leader to team leader and from candidate to candidate. (Currently, interview techniques are inconsistent among team leaders, and they also vary from candidate to candidate.)				
	• Team leaders must prepare for interviews. (Currently, little or no preparation is done.)				
	• Team leaders must structure interviews. (Currently, they just ramble and chat.)				
	• Team leaders must ask well-designed interview questions so candidates' potential fit for production jobs can be assessed accurately. (Currently, questions are not well designed; they are obvious and leading.)				
	• Team leaders must use job-related, legal interview questions. (Currently, they are not familiar with, and do not use, job-related, legal interview questions.)				
	• Team leaders must use objective consistent criteria to make good, well-matched hiring decisions. (Current hiring decisions result in mismatched hires at least 50% of the time.)				

(continued on page 114)

Table 6-2 (continued).

Needs Assessment Stage	Findings	Was Stewart Right (✓)	Was Information New to Stewart (→)?	Training (T) or Non-Training (NT)?	Data Source
Stage 3: Learning Needs	• At the end of the training class, learners must be able to do the following: — Prepare for an interview. — Analyze applications and resumes. — Develop focused, job-related interview questions. — Ask legal interview questions. — Conduct an interview. — Make a hiring decision using objective criteria.				
Stage 4: Learner Needs	• The learners work mostly in teams with their own team or in a team of team leaders; they are not used to working alone.				
	• The fast-paced, stressful environment allows little time to stay focused on one task.				
	• The learners know that they need the training.				
	• The learners are fearful of not doing well in training and being embarrassed.				
	• The learners are not used to sitting in a classroom; they usually move around on the job.				

Findings are the "what" of needs assessment—what is going on. Recommendations are the "how" of needs assessment—how the findings will be used to shape the potential training intervention and other influences so that business and performance needs can be achieved. Chapter 7 focuses on recommendations.

7

Data Analysis Recommendations

What's Inside This Chapter

In this chapter, you'll learn:

▶ More on why it's important to separate the processes of identifying data analysis findings and data analysis recommendations

▶ Developing training recommendations

▶ Developing non-training recommendations

▶ How to make an ROI forecast.

Recommendations Are Not the Same as Findings

The first purpose of a needs assessment study is to determine how a training intervention must affect job performance to meet business needs (training needs). The second purpose is to identify what else must change in the organization to support the desired performance (non-training needs). Both of these purposes should be addressed in the needs assessment recommendations. Chapter 6 addressed both training and non-training findings. This chapter continues with step 5 of the needs assessment process: the development of training and non-training recommendations (see figure 6-1).

Again, it is critical to separate the two thought processes of identifying findings and developing recommendations. You'll recall that data collection planning entails three separate thought processes, and the purpose of keeping them separate is to avoid narrowing down potential choices prematurely.

By the same token, findings and recommendations are separated into two thought processes to avoid the same premature narrowing-down effect. The danger here is that a finding can literally have a recommendation embedded within it, making it easy and tempting to jump to that recommendation. For example, a finding of "Many employees perceive that the benefits program is not as good as other employers' programs" has a potential recommendation embedded within it: "Improve the company's benefits program." This is too easy. Though it could be correct, many times it is not. This finding has to be compared with other findings, patterns and trends must be identified, and the context within which the data was gathered must be analyzed.

Basic Rule 20

Keep the thought process of identifying findings separate from the thought process of developing recommendations.

Making Training Recommendations

Training recommendations are just that: recommendations that the training professional develops to meet the training-related needs that were identified in the needs assessment study. Training recommendations usually include the following areas:

- ▶ the learning objectives for the to-be-developed training course
- ▶ parts of the training course content that should be emphasized or deemphasized to avoid producing a generalized "grab-bag" content set
- ▶ activities to focus on particular skills; because of the needs identified for a particular course/audience, it can be recommended for some content to be addressed simply at the knowledge level, whereas other content that is more important for the purpose at hand should be addressed more deeply and taken to the level of skill practice
- ▶ types of learning activities and training materials (visual, verbal, reference, handouts, notebooks, manuals, and so forth)

- delivery methods (self-study, classroom, classroom plus lab, small group, distance learning, or combinations of these)
- type of learning environment, prework, postwork, prerequisites, training schedule
- audience (type of learners the recommended training is best suited for, depending on their organizational levels, background, experience, and expertise).

Think About This

The nature of training recommendations provides yet another example of how closely training needs assessment is related to training design and how the line between them can become blurred. The entire practice of implementing training—start to finish—is an iterative and interdependent process.

Basic Rule 21
Training recommendations involve all aspects of the proposed training effort.

Making Non-Training Recommendations

Is it the training professional's role to identify non-training issues and make non-training recommendations? Unequivocally, yes. It is appropriate and necessary for the training professional when identifying findings to ask, "What else is going on in the organization that, even if the training program is an unparalleled success, might prevent the attainment of performance and business goals?" It is, therefore, appropriate and necessary for the training professional to develop recommendations to mitigate these non-training issues. Now that this has been said, you may ask why. In answer, there are several reasons:

- Because all the factors affecting job performance are addressed, this comprehensive approach promises the highest likelihood that job performance goals (and, therefore, business goals) will be achieved.

▶ The training effort has the best chance of succeeding in its goals because other contributing factors are addressed as well.

▶ You are focusing on the big picture of job performance, not just on meeting a training need.

▶ You are seen not just as a training provider but as a collaborative internal consultant who enjoys credibility with the client (see chapter 2).

▶ You can build skills as an internal consultant.

▶ Developing non-training recommendations in addition to training recommendations supports survival of the training function (see chapter 2). If the client chooses not to address non-training recommendations, and subsequently the business and performance needs goals are not met, the training effort does not become the scapegoat for the failure. You are on record saying that other factors were involved and should have been addressed.

Basic Rule 22

It is appropriate and necessary to develop both training and non-training recommendations resulting from a needs assessment study.

When findings are identified, the information gleaned is simply that—information. Making recommendations involves deciding what should be done with that information. When the finding is training-related, identifying a recommendation is your job. For example, say a training-related finding is "The learner audience's jobs are fast-paced and highly stressful." A training professional knows that training design must replicate the job environment as much as possible to support transfer. So, in this example the corresponding recommendation might be "Design learning activities so that they are fast-paced and create manageable levels of stress." With non-training-related findings, however, there are more challenges. Not only is the non-training issue not necessarily an area of expertise for the training professional, but it might not be viewed by others as part of the training professional's role to make non-training recommendations.

How to structure non-training recommendations is also a function of the scope, level, and assigned area of the needs assessor's job role and areas of responsibility. Non-training recommendations are also subject to other contextual factors such as the relationship among all of the training and non-training findings that were iden-tified, amount of understanding and willingness on the part of the client to tackle the big picture of performance, and organizational culture.

Challenging as it may be, the case is being made in this book that not only is it appropriate to make non-training recommendations, but it is an essential part of your job. How do you do it? What do you do?

Do you recall the example in chapter 6? A non-training finding was that 80 per-cent of recent ex-employees said that job stress was the primary reason for their leav-ing the organization. At the findings stage in chapter 6, there was no other informa-tion to be gleaned. This information was a fact, and there was no action to be taken at that time. Now, at this stage when you move from findings into recommendations, you must make recommendations regarding what should be done about that fact. Remember, the business need in the example was "to reduce turnover." Here are some possibilities for non-training recommendations related to this finding:

A. Survey current employees to see if they have job stress. If they do, do some-thing to reduce it. If they don't, do nothing.
B. Redesign jobs so that they are less stressful.
C. Do nothing regarding this finding. After all, it was only 30 people who said it out of a large employee population—and they're gone, anyway.
D. Develop a stress management training program.
E. Add benefits that help handle stress—gym membership, for example.
F. Research other patterns in the ex-employee data to see if there might be other patterns among the people who reported job stress (for example, inad-equate employee orientation or other backgrounds/experience in common).
G. Do some research about job stress in the organization to find out how employees define it and what they think causes it.

Which answer do you think is best? All of the above? None of the above? It depends? The correct answer is "It depends," and it depends on four factors:

1. *How this finding relates in context with other training and non-training find-ings:* There may be other indicators in the data that tell you how critical the job stress finding is in the context of the entire needs assessment study.
2. *The training professional's role and level in the organization:* For example, a training professional who is part of an HR department will choose

recommendations differently than a training professional who is part of the operations group because of differences in internal perceptions, organizational hierarchy, and politics. Some of the recommendations would be appropriate for an operations training professional to make but not for an HR training professional and vice versa. If the training professional and client are at the same level in the organization, recommendations will be chosen differently than when the training professional is at a lower level than the client.

3. *Perception of the training function within the organization:* If the training function is already seen as an internal consulting function that focuses on job performance, recommendations will be chosen differently and in a broader scope than in an organization in which the training function is perceived as a training provider on request.

4. *Cost of implementing a recommendation compared to how much benefit will be derived from it:* This factor relates to the process of forecasting the return on the investment in training or non-training interventions.

Deciding upon non-training recommendations and how to position them, then, are very important judgment calls that involve multiple considerations.

So, What About ROI?

Should a return-on-investment (ROI) forecast be part of the recommendations that come out of a needs assessment study? ROI analysis is usually discussed as a part of the training evaluation process. It is an analysis that is calculated after training is complete, and it compares the net benefits of training with the costs of the training.

The ROI calculation is:

$$(\text{Net benefits} \div \text{Costs}) \times 100 = \text{ROI (\%)}$$

Think About This

The entire practice of implementing training—start to finish—is an iterative and interdependent process. The practice of forecasting ROI is yet another example of how closely training needs assessment is related to training evaluation and how the line between them can become blurred.

An ROI of 100 percent means that the training project paid for itself. An ROI that exceeds 100 percent means that the training project produced a return on the initial investment. For example, an ROI of 200 percent means that the training project returned to the organization twice what it cost; an ROI of 1,000 percent means that the training project returned 10 times its cost to the organization.

ROI actually has its beginning in the needs assessment process. One of the ways that training professionals "sell" their clients on the potential value of a training project is by forecasting, or projecting, the potential ROI for the training project. Being able to forecast a positive ROI can be very persuasive; and for some clients, it is the recommendation that convinces them to invest in the project. Following are the steps for establishing an ROI forecast.

Step 1

Calculate the projected value of the business goal. In many cases, the client has already done that for you. For example, an expected increase in sales can be easily translated into a dollar figure; an expected decrease in waste can also be translated easily into dollars. Other, so-called soft measures (for example, customer satisfaction ratings or turnover rates) can have dollar values attributed to them by the specialists who work with those extant data. The HR department, for example, can often tell you what a certain reduction in turnover would save the company. Many marketing departments can tell you what a particular increase in customer satisfaction would make for the organization. For soft measures that have never been calculated, you can use your ingenuity to develop a calculation yourself.

For example, say that you have received a training request for a course for first-line supervisors in how to handle grievances. Your client says that there are too many grievances being escalated past the first-line supervisor stage. When high-level managers and executives have to adjudicate grievances, it wastes their time and the

Think About This

More help in calculating dollar amounts for soft measures is available from several references in the Additional Resources section. Some examples include complaints, customer satisfaction, quality, turnover, absenteeism, morale, and more.

company's resources. You could first calculate an average hourly salary for managers and executives. Then, you could calculate how many grievances are escalated past the first-line supervisor level in a set time period (a quarter, a year) and find out the average number of hours it takes to adjudicate a grievance. If you then multiply the hourly salary times the number of grievances times the average number of hours per grievance, you arrive at the current cost of escalated grievances—the business problem to be resolved.

How much reduction in cost does your client want to achieve? There is no magic formula here. With guidance from historical data and the findings from the current needs assessment study, your client should be able to define a business goal. In this case, how much reduction in cost due to escalated grievances would indicate success to the client? How many fewer escalated grievances does that equal? This discussion results in the *identification of the business goal.*

Step 2

In collaboration with your client, estimate a reasonable proportion of effect that training can be expected to have on the desired business outcome. Building on the previous example, say that X is the current cost of escalated grievances. What percentage of X can you and your client agree on as an expected effect of the grievance training course? Guide your client in thinking about other non-training findings that have been identified as having an effect on the number of escalated grievances (for example, hard-to-understand policies, lack of first-line supervisor desire or motivation to adjudicate grievances themselves, lack of rewards for doing it well, inadvertent "punishment" for choosing not to adjudicate grievances).

There's no magic formula here. Whatever you and your client can agree on as a reasonable estimate is, well, reasonable. In the example, say you and your client reach the conclusion that 20 percent of X is a reasonable expectation for the effect of training. This figure is the *expected benefit* from training.

Basic Rule 23

Work with your client to isolate the expected effects of training through estimates.

Noted

Some people are troubled by the use of estimates in ROI forecasting (in training needs assessment) and calculation (in training evaluation). The fact is that every time people attempt to predict the future in business, they are using estimates—whether setting life insurance premiums or identifying weather patterns that will influence crops. What makes estimates useful in business is, when they are made by people who are experts in that aspect of the business (in this case, your client), they become extremely well-educated estimates. Two important things to remember in identifying ROI estimates with your client: (1) make sure that your client agrees that it is a reasonable estimate; and (2) make sure that you agree that it is a reasonable estimate.

Step 3

Calculate the projected costs of the potential training effort, including needs assessment, design, development, delivery, and evaluation. Here is a list of some costs to consider:

- salaries and benefits of needs assessors, designers, developers, facilitators, support staff
- salaries and benefits of employees who participate in needs assessment
- travel and expenses for all
- contractor's fees
- office supplies and equipment
- purchased materials
- photocopying of materials
- mailing and shipping costs
- salaries and benefits of training participants
- media
- artwork, copyrights, royalties
- training facilities.

Step 4

Calculate the projected ROI:

$$\text{Expected Benefits} - \text{Projected Costs} = \text{Net Expected Benefits}$$
$$(\text{Net expected benefits} \div \text{costs}) \times 100 = \text{ROI (\%)}$$

Step 5

Present the projected ROI as part of your recommendations. Your client may or may not be sold on the training intervention, depending on the projected ROI. There is no magic formula here, either. In some cases, as long as a training intervention pays for itself (100 percent ROI), that's good enough. In other cases, the client may require a substantially positive projected ROI in order to give the "go" order.

Tips for Projecting ROI

Why project ROI at all? Some clients are very bottom-line oriented, and the language of ROI is very meaningful to them. Being able to project ROI shows that you understand your client's need for a bottom-line impact on business measures. Keep these tips in mind as you start to project ROI for your training projects:

- ▶ Level 4 evaluation and ROI are not the same thing. Level 4 involves the business measure itself. In the example, the level 4 business goal is to reduce the number of escalated grievances by 20 percent. The ROI process simply assigns a monetary value to that business measure (number of grievances) and compares it to the costs. ROI, in fact, is often called level 5 evaluation (Phillips, 1997).
- ▶ If the forecasted ROI is less than 100 percent, then you have a training project that will cost more than the expected benefit to the organization. For some clients, you may choose not to include the ROI projection for that reason. Other clients will approve such a project anyway and assume any lost resources as opportunity cost. Other clients will ask that the costs to implement the training project be adjusted to cost less so the ROI can be adjusted higher.
- ▶ When you choose to forecast ROI, you had better achieve it! ROI is a powerful tool for convincing a client that a training project will have impact. It can also cause powerful damage to the training professional's credibility if the expected ROI isn't achieved when the course is evaluated. That's why isolating the expected effects of training, and agreeing on them, is important. What is an acceptable ROI to support a go/no-go decision? That decision is up to your client.
- ▶ There is no rule about what an acceptable ROI forecast is for a training project. That decision depends on your client and how your client chooses to view the many contextual factors that will affect the ROI.

Think About This

Some clients are not interested in ROI, especially insofar as soft measures are concerned. If the goal is to reduce absenteeism by a certain percentage and that reduction occurs, they don't find it necessary to express that achievement in dollars and cents. They are satisfied with the outcome as it is, and there is no need for you to push for an ROI measurement. As Paul McCartney would say, "Let It Be."

"When you get a new hammer, everything in the world looks like a nail." Remember that expression when you think about ROI. This process has become very popular in the training field and for good reason. It is a very powerful, persuasive tool in needs assessment, and a very powerful tool to demonstrate impact in evaluation. It is not, however, the be-all and end-all. It is a way of quantifying the potential benefit of a training intervention. The potential benefit is still there (for example, reduction in number of escalated grievances). The ROI forecast simply translates that potential benefit into a dollar figure so it can be compared with potential costs.

ROI can only be used when all of the other components in the training system are present and support it. If you are not conducting a thorough needs assessment focused on both training and non-training findings, do not forecast an ROI. Likewise, if you are not conducting evaluation levels 1–4, do not calculate ROI during evaluation (McCain, 2005). You will have no interim measures from evaluation levels 1–4 to serve as indicators for making adjustments along the way.

Getting It Done

The goal for a needs assessment study is to produce recommendations. A complete set of recommendations focuses on both training and non-training issues that are affecting the business and performance goals. It is appropriate for the training professional to make recommendations in both areas because the goal is to help the business—not just to have a good training program.

Chris at Whitewater Outfitters is very cognizant of this human performance improvement role and takes it seriously. Check out exercise 7-1.

Exercise 7-1. Whitewater Outfitters case study (part 6).

 Table 7-1 provides the answers to exercise 6-2. Compare your answers to these. If you missed a few of the answers, go back to part 5 of the case and work your way through the findings again.

Chris developed a list of training and non-training recommendations for Stewart (the client) based on the findings. (Remember that Chris is a training professional within the HR department.) Compare your answers from exercise 6-2 with Chris's. Here are Chris's recommendations:

Training Recommendations:
- Design and deliver interview skills training for the team leaders.
  —Learning objectives
    - Prepare for an interview.
    - Analyze applications and résumés.
    - Develop focused, job-related interview questions.
    - Ask legal interview questions.
    - Conduct an interview.
    - Make a hiring decision.
  —Content emphases: legal interview questions, preparation for interviews, how to compare data to make an effective hiring decision
  —Delivery
    - Classroom.
    - Prework (a reading assignment on effective interviewing that learners must read before coming to the class).
    - During the hiring push, convene two or three brown-bag sessions during which learners share what's working, not working, and their questions. They can take that learning back to the workplace immediately to improve their interviews as they continue them.
  —Learning activity parameters:
    - Provide opportunity for "bad" interviewing behaviors to be critiqued in a non-threatening environment (for example, critique the instructor role-playing a bad interview, or critique a video of a bad interview.)
    - Use multiple team-based learning activities. Gradually progress in activities until learners are comfortable working on some activities alone.
  —Process standards
    - Active.
    - Experiential.
    - High energy.
    - Multiple opportunities to practice.
    - Iterative process: Keep circling back to how one subject builds on the last subject.

Non-Training Recommendations:
- Conduct further research regarding the reasons behind the other two EEO complaints. Some other factor is operating here, and correcting the legal aspect of how interviews are conducted will not eliminate the EEO complaints.
- Consider evaluating staffing levels during midday.
- Offer data and assistance to the shipping department in any ways that production might be able to assist.
- Give team leaders more specific reports on causes of customer complaints; offer constructive feedback only on issues that are related to production.
- Coach team leaders not to pass on critical feedback regarding customer complaints that are related to shipping rather than production.
- Consider a comparison of benefits programs between Whitewater Outfitters and Eddie Bean, the other sportswear company in town. If the comparison does not support the employee contention and perception, publicize it. If the comparison does indicate issues, consider conducting a benefits survey to help decide if the benefits program requires revision.

Now Chris must present the needs assessment results to Stewart. What suggestions would you offer Chris in planning and implementing the presentation?

Presentation goals:_____

_____

Audience characteristics: _____

_____

Media and handouts:_____

_____

Presentation style: _____

_____

Information to emphasize: _____

_____

Things to watch out for: _____

_____

Table 7-1.

Needs Assessment Stage	Findings	Was Stewart Right (✓)?	Was Information New to Stewart (→)?	Training (T) or Non-Training (NT)?	Data Source
Stage 1: Business Needs	• The upcoming hiring push will require strong interviewing skills on the part of the team leaders.	✓		T	Waddell (interview)
	• Two of the four EEO complaints in the past fiscal year relate directly to team leaders having asked illegal interview questions.		→	T	Extant data (HR)
	• A glitch in the shipping process has caused 85% of customer and retail store complaints in the past six months. Shipping is not part of the production process.		→	NT	Extant data (complaint department)
	• Turnover is higher than the industry average. There is a direct connection between the higher turnover and the following four factors:	✓			Waddell (interview)
	— Team leaders are making poor hiring decisions, resulting in turnover due to stress and burnout (in underqualified new hires) and boredom (in overqualified new hires).	✓		T	Waddell (interview) and extant data (exit interviews)
	— A common source of stress for all team members occurs during midday hours when fellow team members take lunch breaks and the same amount of work must be done with fewer people on the line.		→	NT	Team leaders
	— Team members are stressed by the large amount of negative and critical feedback they receive from their team leaders regarding the perceived production problems (and team leaders are getting the same negative and critical feedback themselves).		→	NT	Team
	— There is a common perception among employees that Eddie Bean's benefits are better than Whitewater Outfitter's benefits.	✓		NT	Extant (exit interviews) and team leaders

Stage 2: Performance Needs				
• Team leaders must conduct consistent interviews from team leader to team leader and from candidate to candidate. (Currently, interview techniques are inconsistent among team leaders, and they also vary from candidate to candidate.)	✓		T	Interview experts, Waddell (interview), HR extant data, team leaders
• Team leaders must prepare for interviews. (Currently, little or no preparation is done.)		↑	T	Interview experts, Waddell (interview), HR extant data, team leaders
• Team leaders must structure interviews. (Currently, they just ramble and chat.)		↑	T	Interview experts, Waddell (interview), HR extant data, team leaders
• Team leaders must ask well-designed interview questions so candidates' potential fit for production jobs can be assessed accurately. (Currently, questions are not well designed; they are obvious and leading.)		↑	T	Interview experts, Waddell (interview), HR extant data, team leaders
• Team leaders must use job-related, legal interview questions. (Currently, they are not familiar with, and do not use, job-related, legal interview questions.)	✓		T	Interview experts, Waddell (interview), HR extant data, team leaders
• Team leaders must use objective consistent criteria to make good, well-matched hiring decisions. (Current hiring decisions result in mismatched hires at least 50% of the time.)	✓		T	Interview experts, Waddell (interview), HR extant data, team leaders

(continued on page 132)

Table 7-1 (continued).

Needs Assessment Stage	Findings	Was Stewart-Right (✓)?	Was Information New to Stewart (→)?	Training (T) or Non-Training (NT)?	Data Source
Stage 3: Learning Needs	• At the end of the training class, learners must be able to do the following: — Prepare for an interview. — Analyze applications and resumes. — Develop focused, job-related interview questions. — Ask legal interview questions. — Conduct an interview. — Make a hiring decision using objective criteria.	✓ ✓ ✓ ✓	↑ ↑	T T T T T T	Interview experts
Stage 4: Learner Needs	• The learners work mostly in teams with their own team or in a team of team leaders; they are not used to working alone.		↑	NT	Team leaders, prior instructors, prior course evaluation data
	• The fast-paced, stressful environment allows little time to stay focused on one task.		↑	NT	
	• The learners know that they need the training.		↑	NT	
	• The learners are fearful of not doing well in training and being embarrassed.		↑	T/NT	
	• The learners are not used to sitting in a classroom; they usually move around on the job.		↑	NT	

Well, you've reached your goal of producing training and non-training recommendations based on your needs assessment study. Are you finished yet? Not quite! Now you must develop a method to present the data, findings, and recommendations to your client. This task is examined in chapter 8.

8

Communicating
With Your Client

What's Inside This Chapter

In this chapter, you'll learn:

▶ How to plan the presentation of needs assessment study results
▶ Tips for implementing the presentation.

The needs assessment study, data collection, and data analysis are now complete (figure 8-1). Now is the time to present all of this information to your client. It is recommended that you negotiate having a feedback meeting when you present the needs assessment results to the client and discuss them. You can plan to augment the oral presentation with written materials as well.

Planning the Feedback Meeting and Presentation

The discussion that follows addresses the planning process for delivering the information to your client.

Define Your Presentation Goals

Presumably, the goals of your presentation are to (1) persuade the client to give the thumbs-up to the training intervention design and delivery as recommended; and

Figure 8-1. The training needs assessment process with step 6 highlighted.

Step 1. Conduct external and organization scan

Step 2. Collect data to identify business needs

Capitalize on an opportunity
Resolve a problem
Support a strategy

Step 3. Identify potential training intervention

Step 4. Collect data to identify performance, learning, and learner needs

Required performance
Learners' current performance
Required skills and knowledge
Learners' current skills and knowledge
Learner needs

Step 5. Analyze data

Identify findings: gaps in performance, skills, and knowledge
Identify recommendations

Step 6. Deliver data analysis feedback

Training recommendations: design and delivery; ROI forecast
Non-training recommendations: work environment, rewards, consequences, work processes

Transition step: Begin training design

(2) take ownership of the non-training issues and recommendations. As you plan and deliver your presentation, these goals must always be uppermost in your mind. Each comment that you make should draw the audience back to the goals of the presentation.

Basic Rule 24

The goal of the needs assessment presentation is to generate decisions and actions on the part of the client to implement the training project.

Know Your Audience

Who will attend your presentation of findings and recommendations? Will it just be your client or will other key players be invited? Plan to address the interests of all concerned in the presentation. Plan as well to address the audience members' desired level of detail as well. How much information will they want? Are they interested in a short, brief presentation that cuts to the chase? Will they be interested in your methodologies and research?

Separate Findings From Recommendations

Make it clear that findings and recommendations are two separate phases of the project. This fact should be reflected in the outline of the presentation, in handouts and PowerPoint slides, in communications with the client prior to the meeting, and in your own preparation for the presentation. Then, follow through by addressing findings and recommendations separately during the presentation.

Tailor Your Presentation Media and Style

When choosing media for presenting your recommendations and findings and tailoring your presentation style, consider the audience's and your needs.

Your choice of media should be based on its formality and on the types of media your audience tends to expect. Generally speaking, the more self-contained your media are, the more formal they are. For example, PowerPoint is a more formal medium than a flipchart is. If your organization tends to depend on a certain kind of media (for example, PowerPoint), plan to use it at least for transition titles from subject to subject to increase your audience's comfort level.

How formal (or informal) your presentation should be depends on your organization's culture and the client's style. Choose a setting that fits—a boardroom for a formal presentation or a conference table in an office for an informal presentation. Plan to tailor your speaking and presentation style to the level of formality expected.

Think About This

The level of formality of media also tends to imply the potential changeability of the content. When information is printed on a PowerPoint slide, there is a message that the information is not up for revision, that it is carved in stone. Other media—flipcharts or handouts, for example—connote not only less formality, but also less rigidity. Content conveyed this way is deemed by the audience to be more amenable to changes and revisions. For this reason, some needs assessors use multiple media in their presentations: a more formal, "rigid" method to present findings (because these are the facts that you discovered in your study) and a less formal, more easily modified medium for recommendations when the desired message to the audience is "Let's discuss these and revise as needed."

Handout Materials

Consider the level of detail that should go into the handouts and materials that are given to the audience members. Will they want just a brief outline with bullets to fill in with notes? Or will they be looking for text-heavy, highly detailed information? Will they expect a two-page executive summary with just highlights, accompanied by a detailed report? Will graphs and other visual presentation of information be of interest to them?

Structure Your Time

Plan to use no more than half of the allotted time to present findings. The more important part of the presentation is the recommendations. Plus, you should allow sufficient time for your client to digest and discuss the findings, and make the mental transition to recommendations (even perhaps identifying some of the recommendations in the discussion). There is a client readiness factor that must be taken into account before the client is open to discussing and hearing recommendations.

Basic Rule 25

No one loves your methodology and data more than you do! Don't make the mistake of being so enamored of them in your presentation that the recommendations portion is rushed or cut short.

Emphasize Information That the Client Can Affect

Highlight findings that are within the client's power to do something about. You must acknowledge findings that are unfortunate givens in the situation, but emphasizing them only makes the client feel powerless.

Plan Ahead

Well in advance of your presentation, give some thought to what you could cut from the presentation if it becomes necessary. If the client is unexpectedly called away or walks in and says "I know we scheduled an hour, but I'll have to leave in 30 minutes," you'll have to be able to adjust.

Making the Presentation

On some occasions and with some clients, the quality of your presentation can outweigh the quality of the actual needs assessment results. The presentation can be the convincing factor instead of the data. Don't make the mistake of thinking that your data can speak for itself or that the answers are so glaringly obvious that you don't need to point them out.

These are the factors that are most influential in a presentation:

- a level of detail that matches the audience's expectations
- your ability to answer questions that come up during the presentation
- organization of information in such a way as to build evidence, so that the answers logically present themselves to the audience
- your ability to link disparate points of information on the spot, making it obvious to the client that you truly understand the business issues and challenges
- your level of self-confidence.

The more you behave as if "this information is so interesting, and I am sure the trends and patterns are as obvious to you as to me" is more convincing to the client than behavior that communicates "I must convince you that this is correct."

Basic Rule 26

If your client comes up with a recommendation before you present it, that's a good thing!

Also, think about your role in the presentation. During the findings portion of the presentation, your role should be that of an observer; in the words of Sergeant Joe Friday, "Just the facts, ma'am." If the client asks what the data means or what you think about the information, gently and firmly say that this will be addressed in the recommendations portion of the presentation. Later, during the recommendations portion of the presentation, your role can change to that of an advocate for your recommendations.

An apt analogy for this presentation is a courtroom. Your client is the jury who will eventually make a judgment about your testimony. When you are presenting findings, your role is that of an eyewitness: "This is what I saw and heard . . ." The findings are reported to the client with as little bias as possible. When you make the transition from the presentation of findings to recommendations, your role can change to that of an attorney who is actively trying to influence the jury's decisions.

Think About This

The "parking lot" technique that trainers use in training courses can be useful in your needs assessment presentation as well. When a client asks a question that you would like to reserve for the recommendations portion of the presentation, note it on a flipchart or whiteboard and tell that client that this point will be "parked" there until later when it will be addressed.

Steps in the Presentation

1. *Begin with a summary of what was done in the needs assessment study.* Share briefly the methods that were chosen and why, as well as any significant developments that occurred during the data collection.

2. *Present the findings first.* Let them sink in. Ask the client what he or she thinks about a key finding. Allow the client to think through the information. It's possible that the client may arrive at some of the recommendations during the

discussion of the findings. Should this happen, the client's ownership of these recommendations will be assured. When presenting your findings, be simple, concise, and direct. Validate what the client has done right along the way in working on this business need; position your study as augmenting and supplementing the client's efforts. Present new information that contradicts the client's initial presenting problem or beliefs in a "Guess what I found?" mode, not a "You were wrong" mode. Don't try to fill dead air too quickly. Silence on the client's part can mean that he or she is thinking about the data. If the silence becomes uncomfortable, ask the client a question, but don't move on to the next finding yet. Expect some disagreement, rejection, or even disbelief of your information. Let your client digest and assimilate the information you have presented.

Think About This

One helpful technique to try when presenting information that might make the client more comfortable is to use the passive voice. Do you remember this technique from high-school English? With passive voice, the subject of the sentence is acted upon by a cause other than the person who is being addressed. For example, you could say, "There are indications that the initial training program was incomplete," rather than "There are indications that you didn't implement a complete training program." This way, you can avoid using accusatory language (the word "you" is a key offender), giving the client some intellectual distance from the data so that it can be reflected upon, rather than defended against.

3. *Make an obvious transition to recommendations.* Turn the page; change the slide; take a break; make a verbal transition: "Now that we have discussed the findings, I'd like to get into suggestions for what actions we can take based on this information."

4. *Be flexible as the meeting goes on.* If you have prepared well, the flexibility is already built into your plan. Move more quickly or more slowly through information as the needs of the audience require. Change media type if needs dictate. Have a formal PowerPoint presentation ready just in case the audience wants it. Move from PowerPoint slides to a flipchart or whiteboard if the audience wants to generate ideas on the spot.

Think About This

Shifting from, say, PowerPoint slides to a flipchart when you make the transition from findings to recommendations can help make the transition as obvious as possible. The media transition can also give the message that the recommendations are up for discussion and adjustment.

5. *Ask for what you want.* As the presentation winds down, say "Here is what I would recommend that we do." Then itemize: (a) what you will do to begin the design of the training itself; and (b) what you need from the client in the way of addressing (or at least acknowledging) the non-training issues. Together, develop an action plan to outline in a clear and specific way the actions that you both will implement.

Next Steps

You also have to identify non-training issues and recommend what should be done to address them. It is the client's prerogative to determine what actions will actually be taken, if any. Sometimes a client is unable or unwilling to address a non-training issue. In that case, it is imperative that you obtain the client's acknowledgement that the non-training issue exists and that it will affect the achievement of performance and business goals. Do this before you proceed with the training design implementation. At the end of the project when evaluation is implemented, you can point out if necessary that the non-training issue had an effect on desired performance and business goals, and that this was acknowledged at the front end of the project.

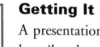

Getting It Done

A presentation of needs assessment findings and recommendations must be tailored to the client's style; be cognizant of the client's business needs; allow opportunity for the client to develop recommendations on his or her own that are then validated in the presentation; and acknowledge the importance of non-training issues that are influencing the business and performance situation.

Exercise 8-1 concludes the Whitewater Outfitters case study.

Exercise 8-1. Whitewater Outfitters case study (part 7).

Following are some of the items that Chris included in the presentation plan. Compare your answers from exercise 7-1 with these. If you identified most of the same responses as Chris, congratulations! If you identified even more implications than Chris, you are clearly in sync with what makes a convincing presentation to a client.

Presentation Needs	Presentation Implications
Presentation Goal	• Obtain Stewart's agreement to implement the training as recommended. • Obtain Stewart's acknowledgment that the non-training issues will have an effect on the attainment of business outcomes.

Client Characteristics	Presentation Implications
Has a strong business need to support the hiring push	• Acknowledge the need up front in the presentation. • Continue to refer back to the business need in the presentation.
Communicated a simpler presenting problem than the needs assessment revealed	• Validate the strong presenting need. • Acknowledge up front that you will deliver interview skills training and that it is an appropriate solution. • Position the needs assessment as a way to tailor the eventual training to the client's situation.
Has other business issues that could be related to the presenting problem	• Continue to refer to other business needs. • Set the stage in the beginning that there may be some other answers for some of the business needs.
Has some assumptions about what training can do that are not accurate	• Provide brief discussion of the role of training in addressing performance issues that are knowledge and skill related.
Was willing to give the benefit of the doubt to the needs assessor and allow access to data sources	• Express sincere appreciation for access to data sources and the client's organization. • Quantify the amount of time and organization resources it took to collect data and express the value of that data to the needs assessment outcomes.
Is sure about what needs to be done	• Continue to acknowledge that interview skills training will take place. • Emphasize that for the interview skills training to be a success, here is what else must be addressed (non-training needs). • Be direct in asking for non-training needs to be addressed.

(continued on page 144)

Exercise 8-1. Whitewater Outfitters case study (part 7) (continued).

Media and handouts	• Be results-oriented; client wants the bottom line. • Offer facts and figures in easily understandable format: graphs, bullets, and so forth. • Continue to refer back to results measures that were presented as part of the problem.
Presentation Style	• Be informal, direct; don't beat around the bush. • Ask client to speculate what each finding means as it is presented; help client own recommendations later.
Information to Emphasize	• Keep coming back to the business and performance needs. • Continue to focus on the non-training issues and recommendations.

Things to Watch Out For	**Presentation Implications**
Has a short timeframe in which to get ready for the hiring push	• Use language of urgency. • Be brief in each section of the presentation.
Has some incorrect assumptions about the causes for the presenting problem	• Validate all the correct assumptions. • Position new and contradictory information as interesting, not contradictory. • Use passive voice when appropriate.

Congratulations! You have now completed the training needs assessment study for Whitewater Outfitters. Now it's time for both needs assessor and client to get to work—Chris to design the training and Stewart to resolve the non-training issues.

This book began "in the middle" because, like it or not, the training professional is often found in the middle of the process—at step 3. Responding to a request for training by stepping back to steps 1 and 2 to place the request in the context of the business needs is the necessary action to take when caught "in the middle." What would it be like if you could start at step 1? Chapter 9 presents that scenario.

The Ideal Organization Scan

What's Inside This Chapter

In this chapter, you'll learn:

▶ What the first two steps of training needs assessment are all about
▶ Sources of external and organization needs assessment information.

Chapter 2 opened with a scenario in which a department manager stops a training professional in the hall and formulates a training request. The training needs assessment approach in this book was based on that scenario because that's the way it happens most of the time in many organizations.

You will remember from the training needs assessment process (figure 9-1) that this scenario depicts the training professional entering the process at step 3 ("Identify potential training intervention"). This scenario requires that the training professional step back into step 1 ("Conduct external and organization scan") and step 2 ("Collect data to identify business needs") to place the potential training intervention in the context of the business needs. That is the approach presented in this book so far. Were you wondering if the true beginning of the process would ever be addressed?

Figure 9-1. The training needs assessment process with steps 1 and 2 highlighted.

Step 1. Conduct external and organization scan

Step 2. Collect data to identify business needs

Capitalize on an opportunity
Resolve a problem
Support a strategy

Step 3. Identify potential training intervention

Step 4. Collect data to identify performance, learning, and learner needs

Required performance
Learners' current performance
Required skills and knowledge
Learners' current skills and knowledge
Learner needs

Step 5. Analyze data

Identify findings: gaps in performance, skills, and knowledge
Identify recommendations

Step 6. Deliver data analysis feedback

Training recommendations: design and delivery; ROI forecast
Non-training recommendations: work environment, rewards, consequences, work processes

Transition step: Begin training design

Now is that time. In a perfect world, training professionals would be able to always engage their clients in a proactive mode. They would consistently and constantly scan the organization (steps 1 and 2 in figure 9-1) for indicators that business needs, performance needs, or both could be addressed by a training-related intervention. Trainers in this perfect world would then approach the potential client with the information gathered and propose a training-related intervention. And, at that point, step 3 would begin, which is where this book and your adventure in needs assessment started!

Think About This

If the perfect-world scenario represents an ideal approach, then why don't more training professionals use it more often? Because these days, training professionals don't have "full plates" of work to do—they have full platters! It is challenging enough to be effectively reactive, which is the approach presented in this book. There are some days when being effectively proactive and scanning the organization seem far out of reach. But, do it as often as possible. Will you ever have a solid week (or even a solid day, for that matter) to conduct a thorough, organized external and organization scan? Not often. So, do it here and there, an hour at a time, an afternoon at a time. Even if you find yourself in reactive mode most often, you will enhance your ability to discuss the business with the client and to couch the expressed training need in the business context.

Organization Scanning and Business Need Identification

Believe it or not, the most important guidelines for steps 1 and 2 of the needs assessment process are simple ones:

- ▸ Keep your eyes and ears open.
- ▸ Read every resource that you can get your hands on.
- ▸ Be a sponge; soak in information even if you don't know at the time how you will use it.

Training professionals are in a unique position in an organization and have access to many informal sources of information about the business and its environment. Employees tell them things that they might not tell others—even their managers.

Trainers are privy to information sharing in other departments when they conduct training. They serve on cross-functional committees and teams and, consequently, have extensive contact with people from other parts of the organization. They work on employee activities, such as annual picnics and so on, and have contacts throughout the organization.

Basic Rule 27

Be a sponge. Soak up information from as many informal and formal sources as possible.

Remember that needs assessment and the resultant training interventions must focus on resolving a business problem, capitalizing on a business opportunity, or supporting a business strategy. As you implement the scanning process, keep focusing on these areas.

Sources of External and Organization Scan Data

As a training professional, you have access to multiple sources of formal information. Ideally, you should interview regularly your main potential clients. How often (monthly, quarterly, yearly) is up to you and your potential clients, but you need to keep your finger on the pulse of their business. Areas to focus on include the client's department mission, departmental strategies, operational goals, plans and objectives, and stated wants and needs.

In the course of your work, make an effort to keep up with such external and internal sources as

- trade and industry journals and newsletters, publications like The *Wall Street Journal, Business Week,* and local and regional newspapers
- your organization's annual report
- competitors' annual reports
- stock market reports, if your organization is publicly traded
- your organization's mission statement
- your organization's strategic plans
- change implementation or reorganization plans regarding equipment, technology, work processes, automation, and business opportunities (new products, service, markets)

- organizational climate indicators (labor/management relationships, grievances, turnover, absenteeism, suggestion box ideas, accidents, short-term sickness, observations of behavior, climate and attitude surveys, and the ever-present gossip and scuttlebutt)
- staffing issues and plans (long- and short-term workforce planning, succession planning, local and national demographics, industry indicators, job function indicators, and population growth)
- efficiency indicators (productivity rates, labor costs, materials costs, product quality, equipment utilization, distribution costs, waste rates, downtime, late deliveries, repairs, operational reviews, customer satisfaction)
- input of potential clients (department heads, managers, and so on)
- reward systems
- input from employees
- extant data from departments that regularly collect their own data (HR, accounts receivable/payable, customer service, quality, and so forth).

Think About This

Most departments that regularly collect extant data shouldn't have a problem allowing you access because your request should be for *aggregate* data only. Training needs assessors don't focus on individual performance issues; those are for individual employees' managers to deal with. For needs assessment, you need aggregate data that (you hope) will indicate trends and patterns for groups of employees.

Think of the external and organization scan as the "Columbo approach." If you remember that famous raspy-voiced TV detective, you'll remember that he was always able to put together seemingly disparate pieces of information and identify patterns that no one else could see. Then the TV viewers would say, "Of course! I see it now!" That's what this approach is about. All the information is out there—it just needs a fresh set of eyes looking at it in a different way. Table 9-1 offers some tips for using the Columbo approach.

Table 9-1. Tips for using the Columbo approach.

	Columbo Action	Ways to Do It
1.	Get out into the organization on a regular basis.	• Eat lunch with different people occasionally. • Take your break in a different break room. • Walk around the production floor and observe (with permission from the manager, of course!). • The only way keeping your eyes and ears open will work is if you are regularly found in different places.
2.	Ask lots of "what" and "how" questions.	• What do you mean by that? • How would this look if it were different? • What's happening that shouldn't be happening? • What shouldn't be happening that is? • How would you solve this if you could?
3.	Think about things in different ways.	• What is the root cause of this? • How does this factor depend on others? • What analogy would capture the way this process looks and feels? • If this problem/challenge were facing a _____, how would they handle it? (Pick an apt metaphor, for example, a baseball team, church choir, Army platoon.)
4.	Keep files of information in a way that makes it easy for you to rearrange them and see patterns.	• Write notes on index cards or in files on your computer that can be copied and pasted. • Maintain a file of clippings from internal and external sources.
5.	Allow yourself thinking time when many patterns and big-picture concepts will occur to you.	• Take a short walk at lunch. • Use 30 minutes to look out the window. • Hang a do-not-disturb sign on your office door for a few minutes each day.

Getting It Done

Now is your chance to think like a trainer in a perfect world. Use exercise 9-1 to brainstorm ways that you can implement the Columbo approach to proactive organization scanning in your work as a training professional.

Exercise 9-1. Identify external and internal resources for conducting performance and business needs scans.

Take a look at the resources listed in the left-hand column. Use the right-hand column to jot down possible specific ideas about how you can access such resources within and without your organization. Where relevant, note the name and position of the resources, or state the location of the source. The first row has a couple examples to get you started, but there's space to add your own ideas.

Resource	Your Ideas
Trade and industry journals and newsletters	• Executive office reception area • Public library • www.makingwidgets.com online newsletter • Public relations officer/corporate headquarters • • • •
National, local, regional newspapers, and magazines	
Your organization's annual report	
Competitors' annual reports	
Stock market reports, if your organization is publicly traded	
Your organization's mission statement	
Your organization's strategic plans	
Change implementation or reorganization plans regarding equipment, technology, work processes, automation, and so forth	
Business opportunities (new products, service, markets)	

(continued on page 152)

Exercise 9-1. Identify external and internal resources for conducting performance and business needs scans (continued).

Resource	Your Ideas
Organizational climate indicators (labor/ management relationships, grievances, turnover, absenteeism, suggestion box ideas, accidents, short-term sickness, observations of behavior, climate and attitude surveys)	
Gossip and scuttlebutt, rumors, and innuendo	
Staffing issues and plans (long- and short-term workforce planning, succession planning, local and national demographics, industry indicators, job function indicators, and population growth)	
Efficiency indicators (productivity rates, labor costs, materials costs, product quality, equip- ment utilization, distribution costs, waste rates, downtime, late deliveries, repairs, operational reviews, customer satisfaction)	
Input of potential clients (department heads, managers, and so on)	
Reward systems	
Input from employees	
Extant data from departments that regularly col- lect their own data (HR, accounts receivable/ payable, customer service, quality, and so forth)	

You may have noticed that there is still one step remaining in the training needs assessment process that has been dissected throughout this book. That is the last step—the transition step from needs assessment into design. It is at this point that the needs assessor switches hats and becomes the training designer or hands the design process over to an instructional designer. It is also the point where this book hands off the reader to other resources for the design process. Some final thoughts are in chapter 10 and lists of references and additional resources follow.

10

A Final Note

- -

What's Inside This Chapter

In this chapter, you'll learn:

▶ The most common errors that can occur in training needs assessment
▶ How strategic needs assessment is related to performance consulting or HPI.

Training needs assessment is the process of identifying how training can help your organization reach its business and performance goals. Often, its most valuable output (to the organization) is the identification of non-training factors that affect these goals. Other outputs include

- ▶ the relationship between stated business and performance needs and the proposed training need
- ▶ the goals at each stage that will ultimately be evaluated in the training evaluation process
- ▶ training design indicators: learning objectives, learning activities, background, and content to help activities simulate the job environment
- ▶ metrics that will be used to measure learning success and business success during the training evaluation process.

Common Errors in Needs Assessment

It would not be right to leave you without a warning about the mistakes you can make in training needs assessment. Following are the most common errors that occur:

- ▶ *Insufficient data collection or analysis:* It could happen that you choose not to conduct a thorough needs assessment or are pressured to cut short these steps by a client. Make it clear at the outset what will be involved in doing a proper needs assessment and get buy-in from your client.

- ▶ *Treating presenting problems only:* It's an error to assume that the client's only issues are the issues that he or she presented and then jump on the bandwagon to resolve those issues. Most of the time, the client's presenting problem is accurate, but it is simply not the only thing that is going on. Needs assessment is the way to ferret out all training and non-training issues.

- ▶ *Applying no tools or the wrong tools:* Always try to triangulate on training and non-training issues by using a variety of data collection methods (at least two). It is also possible to use too many tools, leading to "analysis paralysis."

- ▶ *Trying a quick fix:* Take time to focus on the real problem rather than just treating the presenting problem symptoms.

- ▶ *Applying the wrong fix:* Avoid falling into the trap of just delivering what the client wants rather than what the client needs; sometimes it takes a while to see that "the training request in the hall" was the wrong fix.

- ▶ *Giving feedback in wrong "language":* As a training professional, you're accustomed to using needs assessment or HRD jargon; make an effort to address decision makers in their own unique language (for example, costs, impact, and success).

- ▶ *Assuming one problem/one solution:* Very seldom is a performance or business issue the result of a single problem; there are nearly always multiple issues that require multiple solutions—perhaps a training intervention, perhaps not.

- ▶ *Failing to identify non-training issues:* Whether it is because of pressure from the client, or your own choice, training to reduce a skill deficiency cannot change performance when there are other non-training factors that also affect the performance.

- ▶ *Failing to educate clients regarding non-training issues:* Allowing clients to continue to think that training is the only solution to performance problems does them a disservice because more often than not they won't be able to achieve their business and performance goals. If you don't address non-training issues and fail to close the performance or learning gap, you're doing yourself a disservice and undermining your credibility.

What About Performance Consulting?

Two much-used terms in the HRD field these days are "performance consulting" and "human performance improvement (HPI)". If you have done any reading about these subjects, you may have said to yourself more than once as you have read this book: "How is this needs assessment process different from this performance consulting or this HPI that I have heard so much about? They seem similar." You would be right.

Here's why: Traditionally, training needs assessment has focused solely on identifying the needs relevant to a planned training intervention. That has meant focusing only on data collection and analysis relevant to the content or the method of the training, that is, identifying and quantifying skills to be learned in the training course, learning activities, and learner needs. The focus has always, therefore, been on learning.

HPI is a more comprehensive approach in that it goes beyond just training. Critical components of HPI or performance consulting include (Piskurich, 2002):

- a focus on business and organization goals
- use of a systematic approach based on desired results
- focus on performance accomplishments and performance
- linkage of performance analysis to the job
- analysis of performance gaps
- identification of interventions that will close the performance gaps.

In HPI, there are three types of interventions that can be applied to address performance gaps:

1. *Motivational interventions:* Inserting into the organization various incentives, rewards, and outcomes for desired performance that will influence job performers to choose to perform to standards
2. *Structure/process interventions:* Making changes in organizational structure, reporting relationships, work processes, and procedures to influence job performance and results
3. *Knowledge/skill interventions (training!):* Imparting knowledge and skill to job performers in a way that will improve performance and results.

Sound familiar? It should—it is the approach presented in this book but with a few twists. You might call the approach presented in this book the "HPI training needs assessment approach." Training needs assessment has been presented here as focused on identifying required job performance, ensuring that desired job performance is supported by training, and checking to see that all other factors affecting job performance are also addressed. In responding to a training request, the training professional still begins with the business needs and context, focuses on the performance that is required to meet the business needs within that context, and then refocuses on the learning that must take place to support that required performance. The result of this approach is that the needs assessment study leads to training recommendations (how training interventions should be implemented), and non-training interventions (motivational and structural/process interventions), all of which will support job performance and organization goals.

HPI begins by identifying desired organizational results and performance, and identifies all types of potential interventions. Training needs assessment as discussed in this book begins with desired training results, steps back to place the desired training results in the organizational and performance context, identifies training interventions and other interventions that must help and not hinder the performance.

Perhaps the biggest difference between traditional training needs assessment and the HPI training needs assistance approach espoused here is also the simplest difference. Traditional training needs assessment focuses solely on ensuring that the ultimate training design will support employee performance by gathering information to support the training design, identify and capture skills and knowledge, and ensure that the design replicates the learners' jobs as closely as possible. The HPI training

Noted

Are there occasions when an HPI approach will reveal that only motivational or structural process interventions are necessary and that no training interventions are needed? Yes, but so will this training needs assessment approach. You could conceivably respond to a client's training request by conducting a training needs assessment only to find that the desired performance is being affected solely by non-training issues. Just as in HPI, you would identify these issues and make recommendations to the client.

Basic Rule 28

Call yourself an HPI consultant, a performance consultant, a training professional, or a needs assessor, as you like. Know that what you do has a complete focus on business, performance, learning, and learners.

needs assistance approach goes beyond the training design. It results in recommendations regarding non-training issues that are affecting the achievement of the desired organization and employee performance goals.

Remember that the most important question to ask yourself is this: If the ultimate training program is perfect, what else is going on in the organization that will result in the business needs not being met?

Conclusion

Find ways to make this approach your own. Suggested reading and references are provided in the back of the book to assist you in developing your skills. Remember to be the chicken some days and the egg on other days—use parts of the process as you can to build credibility for your approach. Have confidence in your abilities to expand the perception and role of the training professional in your organization. Remember that when a training program adds value, the training function is valued for its impact and results. A training program adds much more value to the organization when it is focused toward performance improvement and organization results, and when all factors that affect performance and training effectiveness are considered.

References

Block, P. (2000). *Flawless Consulting,* 2nd edition. San Francisco: Jossey-Bass/Pfeiffer.

Fuller, J. (1999). "Understanding Human Performance Improvement." In: B. Sugrue and J. Fuller (editors), *Performance Interventions: Selecting, Implementing, and Evaluating the Results.* Alexandria, VA: ASTD Press.

Mager, R.F. (1997a). *Analyzing Performance Problems,* 3rd edition. Atlanta: Center for Effective Performance.

Mager, R.F. (1997b). *Making Instruction Work,* 2nd edition. Atlanta: Center for Effective Performance.

McCain, D. (2005). *Evaluation Basics.* Alexandria, VA: ASTD Press.

Phillips, J. (1997). *Handbook of Training Evaluation and Measurement Methods,* 3rd edition. Houston: Gulf Publishing Company.

Piskurich, G. (2002). *HPI Essentials.* Alexandria, VA: ASTD Press.

Zemke, R., and T. Kramlinger. (1982). *Figuring Things Out: A Trainer's Guide to Needs and Task Analysis.* Reading, MA: Addison-Wesley.

Additional Resources

██

To support you in your continuous learning, the following list of sources used and additional reference material is provided. The listing of reference material is divided into categories to help you find a source you may need. This is not an exhaustive list by any means; rather, it is a beginning point for you.

Needs Assessment

Bartram, S., B. Gigson, and B. Gibson. (2000). *The Training Needs Analysis Toolkit.* Amherst, MA: HRD Press.

Gupta, K. (1999). *A Practical Guide to Needs Assessment.* San Francisco: Jossey-Bass.

Leatherman, D. (1990). *The Training Trilogy: Assessing Needs.* Amherst, MA: HRD Press.

McClendon, M.J. (2003). *Statistical Analysis in the Social Sciences.* New York: Wadsworth Publishing Company.

Phillips, L. (1994). *The Continuing Education Guide: The CEU and Other Professional Development Criteria,* 3rd edition. Dubuque, IA: Kendall-Hunt Publishing Company.

Phillips, J., and E.F. Holton III. (1995). *In Action: Conducting Needs Assessment.* Alexandria, VA: ASTD Press.

Pike, B. (1994). *Managing the Front-End of Training.* Minneapolis: Lakewood Books.

Rossett, A. (1987). *Training Needs Assessment.* New York: Educational Technology Publishers.

Sparhawk, S., and M. Schickling. (1994, August). "Strategic Needs Analysis." *Infoline,* no. 259408. Alexandria, VA: ASTD Press.

Spencer, L.M., and S.M. Spencer. (1993). *Competence at Work.* New York: John Wiley & Sons.

Sprinthall, R.C. (2002). *Basic Statistical Analysis.* Boston: Allyn & Bacon.

Swanson, R. (1996). *Analysis for Improving Performance.* San Francisco: Berrett-Koehler Publishers.

Adult Learning

Knowles, M. (1990). *The Adult Learner: A Neglected Species,* 4th edition. Houston: Gulf Publishing.

Knowles, M., E.F. Holton, and R.A. Swanson. (1998). *The Adult Learner: The Definitive Classic in Adult Education and Human Resource Development,* 5th edition. Houston: Gulf Publishing.

Merriam, S.B. (editor). (2001). *New Directions for Adult and Continuing Education.* San Francisco: Jossey-Bass.

Merriam, S.B., and R.S. Cafarella. (1998). *Learning in Adulthood: A Comprehensive Guide.* San Francisco: Jossey-Bass.

Vella, J. (2002). *Learning to Listen, Learning to Teach: The Power of Dialogue in Educating Adults.* San Francisco: Jossey-Bass.

Facilitation Skills and Facilitator Competencies

Bentley, T. (1994). *Facilitation: Providing Opportunities for Learning.* New York: McGraw-Hill.

Eitington, J.E. (2001). *The Winning Trainer: Winning Ways to Involve People in Learning,* 4th edition. Boston: Butterworth-Heinemann.

Hunter, D., A. Bailey, and B. Taylor. (1995). *The Art of Facilitation.* Tucson, AZ: Fisher Books.

Justice, T., and D.W. Jamieson. (1999). *The Facilitator's Fieldbook.* New York: AMACOM.

Kearney, L. (1995). *The Facilitator's Toolkit.* Amherst, MA: HRD Press.

Kinlaw, D. (1996). *The ASTD Trainers Sourcebook: Facilitation Skills.* New York: McGraw-Hill.

Leatherman, D. (1990). *The Training Trilogy: Facilitation Skills.* Amherst, MA: HRD Press.

Rumsey, T.A. (1996). *Not Just Games: Strategic Uses of Experiential Learning to Drive Business Results.* Dubuque, IA: Kendall-Hunt.

Shapiro, L.T. (1995). *Training Effectiveness Handbook.* New York: McGraw-Hill.

Wheeling, S.A. (1990). *Facilitating Training Groups.* New York: Praeger.

Instructional Design and Development

Anglin, G. (1991). *Instructional Technology: Past, Present and Future.* Englewood, CO: Libraries Unlimited.

Barca, M., and K. Cobb. (1994). *Beginnings & Endings: Creative Warm-Ups & Closure Activities.* Amherst, MA: HRD Press.

Broad, M., and J. Newstrom. (1992). *Transfer of Training.* Reading, MA: Addison-Wesley.

Carliner, S. (2003). *Training Design Basics.* Alexandria, VA: ASTD Press.

Charney, C., and K. Conway. (1998). *The Trainer's Tool Kit.* New York: AMACOM.

Craig, R. (1987). *Training and Development Handbook,* 3rd edition. New York: McGraw-Hill.

Jones, K. (1997). *Creative Events for Trainers.* New York: McGraw-Hill.

Kolb, D., and D. Smith. (1986). *Learning Style Inventory: User's Guide.* Boston: McBer & Company.

Leatherman, D. (1990). *The Training Trilogy: Designing Programs.* Amherst, MA: HRD Press.

Mitchell, G. (1992). *The Trainer's Handbook: The AMA Guide to Effective Training.* Belmont, CA: Lake Publishing.

Nadler, L. (1989). *Designing Training Programs: The Critical Events Model.* New York. Addison-Wesley.

Newstrom, J.W., and E.E. Scannell. (1980). *Games Trainers Play.* New York: McGraw-Hill.

Newstrom, J.W., and E.E. Scannell. (1991). *Still More Games Trainers Play.* New York: McGraw-Hill.

Newstrom, J.W., and E.E. Scannell. (1993). *More Games Trainers Play.* New York: McGraw-Hill.

Newstrom, J.W., and E.E. Scannell. (1994). *Even More Games Trainers Play.* New York: McGraw-Hill.

Phillips, J., and M. Broad. (1997). *In Action: Transferring Learning to the Workplace.* Alexandria, VA: ASTD Press.

Silberman, M. (1990). *Active Training: Handbook of Techniques, Designs, Case Examples, and Tips.* New York: Lexington Books.

Silberman, M., and K. Lawson. (1995). *101 Ways to Make Training Active.* San Diego: Pfeiffer.

Tracey, W.R. (1992). *Designing Training and Development Systems,* 3rd edition. New York: AMACOM.

Measurement and Evaluation

Brinkerhoff, R.O. (1987). *Achieving Results From Training.* San Francisco: Jossey-Bass.

Dixon, N. (1990). *Evaluation: A Tool for Improving Quality.* San Diego: University Associates.

Kirkpatrick, D.L. (1994). *Evaluating Training Programs: The Four Levels.* San Francisco: Berrett-Koehler.

Phillips, J. (1994). *In Action: Measuring Return on Investment.* Alexandria, VA: ASTD Press.

Phillips, J. (1996). *Accountability in Human Resource Management.* Houston: Gulf Publishing.

Swanson, R., and E. Holton. (1999). *Results? How to Assess Performance, Learning, and Perceptions in Organizations.* San Francisco: Berrett-Koehler.

Performance Consulting

ASTD Press. (2001). "A Guide to Performance." *Infoline,* no. 240101. Alexandria, VA: ASTD Press.

Robinson, D.G., and J.C. Robinson. (1989). *Training for Impact: How to Link Training to Business Needs and Measure the Results.* San Francisco: Jossey-Bass.

Rummler, G. (2004). *Serious Performance Consulting According to Rummler.* Silver Spring, MD: ISPI; Alexandria, VA: ASTD Press.

Silberman, M. (editor). (2001). *The Consultant's Tool Kit.* New York: McGraw-Hill.

Willmore, J. (2004). *Performance Basics.* Alexandria, VA: ASTD Press.

Presentation Skills

Becker, D., and P.B. Becker. (1994). *Powerful Presentation Skills.* Chicago: Irwin Professional Publishing.

Burn, B.E. (1996). *Flip Chart Power: Secrets of the Masters.* San Diego: Pfeiffer.

Jolles, R.L. (2000). *How to Run Seminars and Workshops: Presentation Skills for Consultants, Trainers, and Teachers.* New York: John Wiley & Sons.

Peoples, D.A. (1997). *Presentations Plus: David Peoples' Proven Techniques* (revised edition). New York: John Wiley & Sons.

Pike, R., and D. Arch. (1997). *Dealing With Difficult Participants: 127 Practical Strategies for Minimizing Resistance and Maximizing Results in Your Presentations.* San Francisco: Jossey-Bass.

Rosania, R. (2003). *Presentation Basics.* Alexandria, VA: ASTD Press.

Silberman, M., and K. Clark. (1999). *101 Ways to Make Meetings Active: Surefire Ideas to Engage Your Group.* San Diego: Pfeiffer.

Stettner, M. (2002). *Mastering Business Presentations.* McLean, VA: The National Institute of Business Management.

Zelazny, G. (1999). *Say It With Presentations: How to Design and Deliver Successful Business Presentations.* New York: McGraw-Hill Trade.

Strategic HRD

Chalofsky, N.E., and C. Reinhart. (1988). *Effective Human Resource Development.* San Francisco: Jossey-Bass.

Gilley, J., and A. Maycunich. (1998). *Strategically Integrated HRD: Partnering to Maximize Organizational Performance.* Reading, MA: Addison-Wesley.

Hudson, W. (1993). *Intellectual Capital: How to Build It, Enhance It, Use It.* New York: John Wiley & Sons.

Sevenson, R., and M. Rinderer. (1992). *The Training and Development Strategic Plan Workbook.* Englewood Cliffs, NJ: Prentice Hall.

Walton, J. (1999). *Strategic Human Resource Development.* London Guidhall University: Financial Times/Prentice Hall.

About the Author

■ ■

Deborah D. Tobey has 20 years of experience in the HRD field and is principal of a solo consulting practice in human and organization performance improvement, DEB TOBEY LLC. She works with client organizations in consulting skills development and consulting systems; training needs assessment, design, facilitation, and evaluation; strategic planning; teambuilding; group process consultation; competency modeling; and leadership development. Her clients include *Fortune* 500 organizations in manufacturing, finance, import, health care, and the service sector, as well as nonprofit organizations, state and local governments, and universities.

Tobey functions often in a mentor/coaching role with HRD professionals and students. She has served ASTD in several officer capacities since 1986. She has a bachelor's degree in English and a master's degree in student personnel administration and counseling, both from Virginia Tech. Her doctorate in HRD is from Vanderbilt University. She served for four years as adjunct professor of the practice in HRD at Vanderbilt University and is currently an adjunct professor in the HRD graduate program at George Washington University. She is co-author of *Facilitation Basics,* another book in ASTD's *Training Basics* series.

She lives in Nashville, Tennessee, with her husband, Bryan Tobey. Deborah D. Tobey may be reached at dtobey@mindspring.com or www.debtobey.com.